THE
GRAND PRIX COMPANION

THE
GRAND PRIX COMPANION

1906

- ALAN HENRY -

ICON BOOKS

Published in the UK in 2007
by Icon Books Ltd, The Old Dairy,
Brook Road, Thriplow,
Cambridge SG8 7RG
email: info@iconbooks.co.uk
www.iconbooks.co.uk

Sold in the UK, Europe, South Africa and Asia
by Faber & Faber Ltd, 3 Queen Square,
London WC1N 3AU
or their agents

Distributed in the UK, Europe, South Africa and Asia
by TBS Ltd, TBS Distribution Centre, Colchester Road
Frating Green, Colchester CO7 7DW

Published in Australia in 2007
by Allen & Unwin Pty Ltd,
PO Box 8500, 83 Alexander Street,
Crows Nest, NSW 2065

Distributed in Canada by
Penguin Books Canada,
90 Eglinton Avenue East, Suite 700,
Toronto, Ontario M4P 2YE

ISBN-10: 1-84046-796-7
ISBN-13: 978-1840467-96-3

Typesetting and design by Oliver Pugh

Printed and bound in the UK by Clays of Bungay

CONTENTS

INTRODUCTION

This book evolved progressively over several detailed debates with my publisher, Oliver Pugh, and has continued to evolve even as it was being written. What we started out trying to deliver was a random selection of facts, figures, stories, anecdotes and general gossip from my 33 years covering the F1 championship. Yet at the same time here at last was an opportunity to share with a wider audience some of the F1 Shaggy Dog Stories with which I have regaled my journalistic colleagues in press rooms across the world, doubtless much against their will.

I hope the end result will make you smile. Between these covers you'll discover another facet to the life of Britain's most colourful world champion, James Hunt; hear how a French journeyman told the legendary Ayrton Senna precisely where he could get off; learn about Niki Lauda's piloting skills; and hear how Frank Williams conned the author into giving him a lift to the circuit to find out a few fruity facts about what FIA president Max Mosley got up to in his life before becoming boss of the sport's governing body. There is also a selection of random F1 statistics to — hopefully — keep you amused, together with profiles on all the world champions and a fair few others, drivers and team owners, besides.

I would like to thank Ben Clissitt, the sports editor of *The Guardian*, for which I've worked these past twenty years, for permitting me to reproduce a feature I wrote for them on the components that go into making a Grand Prix car. I would also offer my appreciation to Chas Hallett, editor of *Autocar*, Matt Bishop, editor-in-chief of *F1 Racing*, plus Justin Hynes and Norman Howell of the *Red Bulletin* — F1's enormously popular and subversive 'school magazine' — for allowing me to reproduce columns from their respective publications. Thanks also to fellow media centre occupants Nigel Roebuck, Maurice Hamilton and Eric Silbermann, on whom many of these recollections and anecdotes have been tested — arguably to destruction — prior to publication.

Alan Henry
Tillingham, Essex
October 2006

THE
GRAND PRIX COMPANION

SO WHAT IS THE FIA AND WHY DOES FORMULA 1 NEED IT?

Right, we'll start this volume with the really complicated question. If you're too close to the F1 business you might well simply reply 'God alone knows'. If you're a contemporary F1 team principal, you'll probably start hyper-ventilating or perspiring, or suddenly feel in need of a good long sit down to get your blood pressure under control.

After a few moments to compose himself, the flustered team boss might reply: 'Because the sport historically needs an independent regulator.' Of course what he really means —

but doesn't dare say out loud, at least not on the record — is that without the FIA there would be no platform from which Max Mosley, the governing body's controversial president, could spend his time aggravating the hell out of all the participants. Tee, hee, just my little joke, you understand. Well, they *might* say that. But not if they wanted to avoid being ambushed by some unexpected heartache a little further down the road. And yet the whole *raison d'être* for the FIA's existence is, understandably, more complex than that.

Quite why the French originally ended up running motor racing is one of those historical quirks lost in the mists of time. The Fédération Internationale de l'Automobile, commonly referred to as the FIA, is a non-profit organisation which was established on 20 June 1904 to represent the interest of motoring organisations and car users. That's just about two years before Ferenc Szisz won the very first Grand Prix at the wheel of a Renault. So that's quite a long time ago, then.

In 1922 the FIA delegated the organisa- tion of motor racing to the CSI (Commission Sportive Internationale) which later became the FISA (Fédération Internationale du Sport

Automobile) and in 1993 a restructuring of the FIA led to the disappearance of the FISA, thereby placing motor racing under the direct control of the FIA.

So What Sort of an Organisation is the FIA?

Well, you'd have to say that up to the late 1970s it was a pretty benign sort of set-up, like an elderly uncle snoozing in the corner after a good Sunday lunch, just occasionally waking up to throw the odd squib into the debate before drifting off again.

Yet as early as the end of 1958 we got a taste of what the governing body could do. At a reception to celebrate Mike Hawthorn's world championship, the FIA's elderly president Auguste Perouse stood up and announced that, as from the start of 1961, the F1 engine regulations would be reduced from 2.5 to 1.5 litres. The Brits reacted with howls of dissent and pretended to ignore the new rules in the hope that they might go away.

They didn't, and so Ferrari — who'd

publicly tut-tutted with the rest of them while working flat-out behind the scenes on a new 1.5-litre V6 engine — duly won the '61 championship in convincing style.

Yet almost so as to prove that there's nothing new under the sun, the FIA's motorsport interests were catapulted back into the forefront of attention from 1979 when the newly elected president, Jean-Marie Balestre, pledged to reduce the influence of Bernie Ecclestone and the Formula 1 Constructors' Association (FOCA) which — he judged — now wielded far too much power.

Truth be told, this was simply a spat over who controlled the enviable — and ever-increasing — income streams from within the F1 business. The battle was finally resolved by the signing of the Concorde Agreement which has formed the framework by which F1 has been administered ever since 1981. This was only a qualified success for Balestre, as the FISA — as it then was — gained only a small percentage of the television coverage and circuit publicity rights, most of which continued to accrue to FOCA.

Balestre's thirteen-year stint as the most powerful man in motorsport finally came to

an end in the autumn of 1991. Having last
faced a challenge to his FISA presidency ten
years earlier, when Britain's RAC representa-
tive Basil Tye was roundly beaten off, Balestre
had been elected unopposed on two subsequent occasions.

However, that all came to an end in
October 1991 when British lawyer Max Mosley,
one of the founders of race car manufacturer
March Engineering and by then president
of the FISA Manufacturers' Commission,
toppled him by 43 votes to 29.

So what did we all think of Max Mosley?
Well, taking the charitable viewpoint, he tried
to maintain a degree of balance between the
high-spending manufacturer-backed F1 teams
and the smaller independent operations. But
when he championed the notion of fixed-
specification, long-life F1 engines to be
introduced from the start of 2007, many
people felt that he'd gone too far and that
the 'dumbing down' of motorsport's most
senior category had spiralled out of control.

This is my 'Rumble Strip' column from
the September 2006 issue of *F1 Racing* in which
I tried to place this complex dilemma in its
true perspective:

Back in the 1980s Maggie Thatcher put the full force of her political clout behind the poll tax. The Iron Lady believed that she knew best and was determined to force it through despite grave misgivings from even members of her own Conservative party — not to mention demonstrations in the street. She had to back-track and although she remained in office for some time, she was fatally holed beneath the waterline. From that point on the clock was ticking on her political future.

It is my mounting belief that homologated fixed-spec FI engines may come to be seen as the equivalent of the poll tax as far as Max Mosley is concerned. The FIA president clearly believes that his overall strategy and vision for the future of FI is calculated to save its commercial prospects. He thinks that homologated engines will make the sport more affordable, thereby ensuring its continued rude health.

On August 7, while holidaying at his villa on the Côte d'Azur, Mr Mosley received GPMA [Grand Prix Manufacturers' Association] plenipotentiaries Dr Burkhard Goeschel and Dr Juergen Reul to effectively sign what amounted to the car makers' document of capitulation. If the FIA have moved their position much on this, then you'd have needed a microscope to discern it. Despite thinly veiled threats of possible arbitration the game seemed to be over.

The car manufacturers under their GPMA grouping have been laughably inefficient when it has come to tackling the FIA. Their proposals have been ridden with ambiguities, poorly presented and they have demonstrated all the negotiating agility of a fully laden oil tanker in a Force 10 gale. Small wonder that the intellectually superior Mr Mosley thinks he can run rings around them. But of course this is not the point. The hard facts of the matter is that everybody in the F1 business has been looking in totally the wrong direction.

Obviously the engine regulations provide a key cornerstone on which the technical rules are constructed. But the notion that the paying public will somehow admire the concept of an engine the specification of which is fixed for three years strikes me as missing the point as to why we all trudge around the world reporting on a sport which we love and which we should all remember is supposed to be an entertainment, first and foremost.

If Mr Mosley had focused his heady cocktail of charm and intimidation more on sorting out the aerodynamic regulations then we might be very much closer to solving the sport's most nagging problem — just why cars don't overtake very much any longer. Which is why an increasing number of fans seemed to be turned off by what most of us still hold dear as the greatest sport in the world.

It was once written that every public meeting should have somebody at the back heckling the platform and shouting 'balls' at the speakers concerned. When I saw the finalised long-term F1 engine regulations I felt that here was a role for me in the unlikely event I could gatecrash an FIA World Council Meeting.

When Mr Mosley was first elected as FIA president in 1991 there was an overwhelming feeling of a bright new day dawning after the volatile years under Jean-Marie Balestre. He promised a light touch, repeatedly assured us that he would not be an interventionist President, that F1 could pretty well run itself and that he had other things to do. To be fair, initially he kept to his word, but he now dabbles unceasingly. These days the FIA seems to operate with a Nanny-knows-best mentality.

Perhaps Mr Mosley does, of course. But then Maggie Thatcher thought that too. And look what happened to her.

Things You Didn't Know About Max Mosley, the FIA President

• As a teenager he was expelled from his boarding school in Germany after what he describes as a 'slight misunderstanding'. Actually he was caught red-handed in the girl's dormitory. Nice work if you can get it, as they say.

• His father, the controversial pre-war politician Sir Oswald Mosley, had problems getting the family passports reinstated after the Second World War. The whole family, including nine-year-old Max and his ten-year-old brother Alexander, finally sailed away from England to Portugal in 1949 in a 60-ton ketch which his father had bought for their 'escape'.

• Max did more than a dozen parachute jumps when he was a member of a parachute regiment in the Territorial Army during his national service in the late 1950s.

• On 31 July 1962, while reading for his Bar examinations (and no silly jokes about whose round it is, please), he was with his father at a political meeting in Ridley Road, Dalston — a tough area of East London — when Sir Oz was 'knocked down and pummelled'. Max, to his credit, waded in to help his father — and ended up getting arrested. The following day Max defended himself ably before the magistrates and was acquitted.

• He was racing his own private Formula 2 Brabham in the 1968 race at Hockenheim in which the legendary Scottish driver Jimmy Clark was killed.

• When Max started race car manufacturer March Engineering in 1969, in partnership with Robin Herd, Alan Rees and Graham Coaker, Sir Oswald told him: 'You'll almost certainly go bankrupt, but it will be good training for something serious later on!' Prescient, or what?

LITTLE BIG MAN

Bernie Ecclestone makes a very good friend and a very bad enemy. One of Britain's richest residents with a personal fortune estimated in excess of £4bn, he is a man who always keeps his rivals guessing. He is a dealer and a gambler who knows that the first rule of business is never to let your rivals know what you are thinking, let alone what you are about to do next.

Behind Ecclestone's impassive public demeanour is a burning competitive spirit. He's not just a businessman. He's a racer. A straightforward businessman may take risky decisions, but racers like Ecclestone live right on the edge. And just as he was in the days when he owned the Brabham team, he wanted to have his finger on the pulse of every aspect of the operation.

'Oh God yes, he could be an interfering bastard', said Charlie Whiting, the FIA race director and safety delegate who was chief mechanic at Brabham when Ecclestone owned the team. 'He was always standing on the pit wall with a couple of stopwatches he didn't know how to work. Then he would lose track, mutter "fucking stopwatches" and throw them down. But yes, he did like to be involved.'

In particular, Whiting recalled the 1987 San Marino GP when Riccardo Patrese was running second in the Brabham BT56 'which was pretty good for a Brabham in those days. He needed new tyres, but Bernie wouldn't let him stop.

'Then his team-mate Andrea de Cesaris was getting frantic. "I wanna come in, I wanna come in!" he was shouting over the radio. And Bernie was shouting "no, stay out, stay out". And I'm going: "Bernie, for Christ's sake, he's got to stop for tyres, they're screwed!" In the meantime Andrea was getting more and more emotional. Eventually he came in for tyres with about five or six laps to go, I think, went straight out again and immediately crashed the car because he was so stressed out by it all.

'So I think perhaps Bernie got a little more deeply involved than he should have done, but at the end of the day it was his bat, his ball and he wanted to play the game exactly as he saw it.'

That has always been the way. In the 1950s he made a fortune as a car dealer in London's notorious Warren Street area and later expanded to smart premises in Bexleyheath, the area in which he had grown up after his family moved from Suffolk where he was born. Even as a schoolboy he was buying and selling:

pens, cakes, anything in demand. And he always wanted to be in control. 'Delegation is the art of accepting second best' would become one of his favourite phrases.

Watching Ecclestone working the F1 paddock is like watching a priest presiding over his flock. He shimmers from team to team, his uniform of Emporio Armani white shirt, dark slacks and black loafers unvarying from day to day. A touch on the shoulder, reassuring or intimidating, depending on your status, a grin, a brief pause for a quick exchange of pleasantries. Then off to the next appointment.

On a personal level, Ecclestone is a private man. He lives in a Chelsea mansion only a few minutes' drive from his offices in Princes Gate, overlooking Hyde Park. He surrounds himself with a tight coterie of trusted acolytes, many of whom have worked for him ever since the Brabham days. To them he will always be Bernie, only Mr Ecclestone on the most formal of occasions.

Ecclestone, his wife Slavica and their daughters Tamara and Petra have all the accoutrements which go with serious wealth: the private jets based at Biggin Hill, the former fighter aerodrome which he owns, the super yacht in the Mediterranean, and the luxury cars. Yet somehow Ecclestone manages to keep his image low-key, almost unobtrusive. It is a clever balancing act.

Formula 1 without Ecclestone seems an unlikely prospect until the inevitable force of gravity finally takes its toll. But any journalist who has asked him, albeit tentatively, what happens after he's gone, will report that the reply is always the same. 'I'm not *going* anywhere.'

Gerhard Berger on Ayrton Senna

'We pushed each other really hard, but he was just so quick that you couldn't believe it', said Gerhard. 'I started the first race of my McLaren career on pole position, so I thought "this is OK, this guy can be beaten". After that I hardly ever saw which way he'd gone.

'If Ayrton hadn't been killed in 1994, F1 would have entered probably its dullest period ever. He'd have been on pole position all the time, won every race for years and taken four more world championships with Williams through to the end of 1997.

'We were the about same age and he was a great guy. I wouldn't have missed racing with him for the world. He taught me how to be a professional and I like to think I taught him how to laugh.'

DEATH OF A PLAYBOY

Johnny Servoz-Gavin, who died at the age of 64 on 29 May 2006, forged a reputation as one of France's most promising young F1 drivers, although his fleeting career saw him compete in only twelve world championship Grands Prix before abruptly deciding to retire after failing to qualify his Tyrrell team March 701 for the 1970 Monaco race.

The high spot of his career came in the 1968 Italian GP at Monza, where he was competing as Jackie Stewart's team-mate in Ken Tyrrell's Matra International squad.

After Stewart retired his Matra-Ford MS10 with engine failure, Servoz-Gavin kept his sister car in the thick of the high-speed battle all the way to the chequered flag, and just pipped the Ferrari of Jacky Ickx for second place behind Denny Hulme's McLaren.

Georges-Francis Servoz-Gavin was born in Grenoble and became universally known as 'Johnny' from his days as a teenage ski instructor on the slopes above his home town. With his long blond hair and easy manner, the young Frenchman was hugely popular with the ladies and quickly developed something of a playboy image which he never quite managed to shrug aside.

'Johnny Servoz' was an unrepentant hell-raiser who burned the candle at both ends. He managed to blow himself up twice for the same reason — cleaning the engine of his boat with petrol while puffing away happily on a Disque Bleu. He survived on both occasions!

The Way We Were

In the mid-1960s, the impecunious Frank Williams used to scrounge a sofa in a motor racing flat in London's Lower Sloane Street on which to sleep.

The brethren eventually decamped to less

salubrious premises in Pinner Road, Harrow. This soon became a clearing house for the British motorsports fraternity, and it also enabled Frank to expand his social circle from his previous position as a salesman for Campbell's Soup, a task he found — and we think you'll like this — too gruelling.

Through aspiring racer Jonathan Williams — no relation — he met such diverse characters as Charlie Crichton-Stuart, grandson of the fifth Marquess of Bute, whose family owned much of Cardiff city centre; Charles Lucas, the son of a Yorkshire landowner, and wheeler-dealer Anthony Horsley, 'Bubbles' to one and all. By then he'd already come to know Sheridan Thynne, a member of the Marquis of Bath's family, David Brodie and Piers Courage, the brewery heir who would come to play such a pivotal and unforgettable role in Frank's future life.

Charlie Crichton-Stuart, who sadly died after a heart attack in 2001, aged barely 60, told the author that Jonathan Williams's view about Frank's aptitude as a mechanic was bang on target. 'He had none at all, absolutely zero', said Charlie.

'He also claims the first time he did

anything for me was when I asked him to do an oil change on my Cooper F3 car. I can't remember whether that's right, but I'm sure it is. I wouldn't have had the faintest idea what an oil union was, anyway. Frank had obviously advanced to the level where he could take a sump plug out, well ahead of my capability.'

Brodie recalls a mark of manhood which had to be displayed by every one of the Pinner Road brigade on their arrival by car. 'It was a matter of honour that you had to park outside in the most spectacular manner possible', he said. 'Best of all was Piers Courage who used to lock up his Zodiac in second gear from about 400 yards' range and would then spin it to a halt neatly in the parking bay, before emerging to charm us all with that unforgettable sunny smile of his.

'I tried to master this technique and ended up half spinning and taking out a nearby privet hedge. Frank, meanwhile, dismissed us as "all wankers". Then one Saturday afternoon we were all sitting around the television watching the wrestling with Kent Walton, as we did, when we heard this horrendous skidding noise from somewhere outside.

'Bubbles just looked up and murmured "too fast" in his soft, deadpan voice. Then we heard another screech followed by a "whoompf" and then another "whoompf". We rushed out to see a Fiat 500 neatly parked on its side in the bay, then its driver's door opened like the hatch on a submarine and Frank, wearing that ridiculous, oversized costermongers' cap of his, climbing out grinning like an idiot.'

The young Williams would always do *anything* for a bet, as Charlie Crichton-Stuart recalled. He bet Frank 10 shillings (50p) that he wouldn't run, stark naked, across the road outside the flat on a Sunday morning when the congregation was leaving the church next door to the flat.

'We locked the door by the time he returned', said Charlie. 'But Frank being Frank, he called our bluff. The future world championship F1 team owner went back into the middle of the road and started leaping about like a dervish, beating his fists on his chest, with us all hanging out of the window pleading for him to come in again.'

A Man of His Word — But Listen Carefully!

Bernie Ecclestone has gained a reputation as being a man of his word. But you'd better listen carefully. Jackie Oliver, the one-time owner of the now-defunct Arrows F1 team, remembered how the teams tried to oppose Ecclestone's move to introduce refuelling in 1994 in order to spice up the television show.

'We were all saying we didn't want refuelling and anyway the refuelling rigs were going to be very expensive', said Oliver. 'So he said "OK, I'll supply the rigs" and we all accepted that. The next thing was that we were invoiced for them. So we rang Bernie and said "We thought you were going to supply these refuelling rigs?" And he replied "I said I was going to supply them, I didn't say that I was going to pay for them."

'So you have to pay close attention to his choice of words. He is a good compromiser who will leave himself negotiating room. But you have to listen to what he doesn't say as much as what he does.'

THE EVOLUTION OF THE F1 CAR

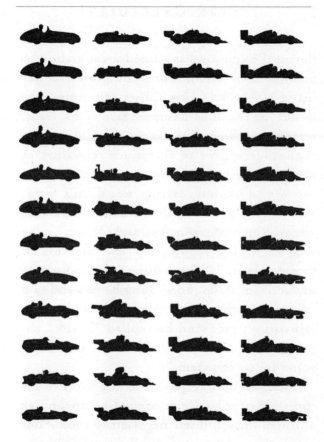

Above is a selection of championship-winning cars and their drivers from the first 50 years of Grand Prix racing. Can you guess who they are?

WATCH YOUR WASTE
PAPER BASKETS!

Bernie Ecclestone's talents were quickly identified by Max Mosley as long ago as 1970, when Max was team manager of the fledgling March F1 squad and Ecclestone was just in the process of buying the rival Brabham team. They became collaborators at meetings of the emergent Formula 1 Constructors' Association, which Bernie would use as the foundation for his expanding power base through the following decade.

'Bernie was an ace negotiator', Mosley remembered. 'I learned all the tricks of the trade from him. One of those was that, if one wanted to adjourn a meeting for a private discussion, my technique was to politely offer to leave the room and leave the other side to consider its position.

'Bernie's strategy was to force the other side to leave the room so that he could rifle through the waste paper basket and read all the notes they'd written to each other while they were negotiating.'

Women at the Wheel. Why Haven't We Had More of Them?

Only a handful of women have even attempted to make the grade in F1, and only a single one managed to score a world championship point — well, at least half a point! Lella Lombardi — who sadly died of cancer in 1992 at the age of 49 — drove a works March-Cosworth to sixth place in the 1975 Spanish GP at Barcelona's Montjuich Park circuit.

Disappointingly for her, the race was stopped prematurely due to a major accident, with the result that only half points were awarded right down the field. The other lady driver to compete on a semi-regular basis was Maria-Theresa de Fillipis, who raced a Maserati in the late 1950s, while South African Desire Wilson at least had the distinction of winning a non-title British national F1 race in 1980, but failed by a whisker to qualify her private Williams FW07 for the British GP at Brands Hatch.

Italian girl Giovanna Amati tried without success to qualify a Brabham BT60 for a handful of races at the start of 1992 — her replacement Damon Hill did rather better.

Problems with upper body strength in the high lateral-G environment of an FI cockpit are the reasons usually attributed to this lack of female single-seater achievement. But American girl Danica Patrick — eighth in the 2006 Indianapolis 500 — and Brits Katherine Legge and Susie Stoddart — in Champcar and DTM (the prestige German touring car series) respectively — are out to prove otherwise!

AYRTON SENNA STORIES

Three cameos to offer a remarkable insight into the cerebral Brazilian driver who won three world championships.

- 1984 -

It wasn't Senna's sheer speed which made the biggest impression on the Toleman-Hart team during his freshman FI season in 1984 — it was his supreme confidence. Here was this 23-year-old, fresh out of Formula 3, ringing up Brian Hart to quiz him on the detail of the turbo 1.5-litre engines which the team would be using.

Brian recalled with respect and admiration: 'He rang me up in the winter. He said: "This is Ayrton. As you know, Alex Hawkridge [the team principal] has signed me. I want to know all about the engine, what boost we're going to use and how I should drive it." This approach was absolutely characteristic of his determination to understand every detail of the car he would race. What an incredible guy. As well as being unbelievably quick, he was the complete dedicated racing driver.'

It didn't take long for the entire Toleman team to work out that Ayrton's emerging talent was growing at a much faster rate than their team. They all realised that this young Brazilian guy was going all the way to the top — and the fact which absolutely convinced them of this reality was his run to third place in the British Grand Prix at Brands Hatch, where he decisively out-drove several people whom he had no right to be ahead of in the car/engine combination that was the Toleman TG184.

After Brands Hatch, Ayrton really held the whole team together. Brian built some special engines and the team really thought they would blitz their way to a maiden Grand Prix win. Ayrton said it felt easy. He was running right up with Niki Lauda and the rest of the front runners in the German Grand Prix. Then the rear wing broke.

Ayrton came back to the Toleman motorhome in a very pensive mood, but although he was upset that the car had broken, he was even more disappointed at losing the opportunity to show what he could do. Everybody in the team suddenly realised that their great Brazilian protégé had begun to appreciate that he would have to switch teams in 1985 if he was to make any serious progress.

His essential honesty also made a big impact on both Hart and Hawkridge. After finishing third in the Portuguese GP behind the McLarens of Prost and Lauda, Senna stayed on for a test session at Estoril. The following day he arrived at the track and said to Hart: 'I want to ask you a question — am I doing the right thing going to Lotus?' Brian told him that he definitely was making the right decision. Renault and Lotus understood more about turbocharged engines and the whole F1 business in general.

Senna told Hart just how difficult it was

for him to leave Toleman. Then he went out in the TG184, lapping two-tenths of a second quicker than he'd managed in qualifying for the race. He even had time to wave to Brian as he rounded the hairpin. What a star!

- 1985 -

Was Senna heavy on fuel? That was one of the key questions being asked mid-way through his debut season with Lotus in 1985. It appeared that his Lotus 97T's tanks ran dry in both the San Marino GP at Imola and during the British GP at Silverstone. But in fact, neither was the case. At Imola his car had been fitted with the less fuel-efficient Renault EF4 engine rather than the newer and more economical EF15, and at Silverstone a broken sensor in the electronic management system caused one bank of cylinders to move onto 'full rich', destroying his carefully planned race strategy.

Senna recalled Silverstone as one of his most satisfying races, even though it did not produce the firm result expected. 'If you have a good race, then you enjoy yourself', he reflected. 'At Silverstone in 1985 my Lotus was running really well. OK, it failed to finish, but I came away satisfied because I had been running strong and fast, in complete control of what I was doing.'

This was revealing, because it emphasised the fact that Senna was interested only in measuring his achievements by his own standards. The opinion of outsiders meant little. He contrasted the Silverstone race with his flat-out run to third place in the '86 Monaco GP, where he finished behind the McLaren-TAGs of Alain Prost and Keke Rosberg.

'Sure I was on the podium in third place behind the two McLarens', he conceded, 'but the car was a disaster to drive and it was a tremendously hard race. I did not feel particularly happy about it.'

Ironically, in 1985 he was to dominate the opening stages at Monaco, but paid the long-term penalty for momentarily over-revving his engine in the race morning warm-up. The team, already flat out changing an engine in team-mate Elio de Angelis's car, asked him if he would race it anyway. Ayrton did so, but he was sufficiently shrewd to realise that he had done damage to the engine which was potentially terminal. And so it proved.

Senna's performance in 1985 convinced him that Lotus did not have the resources to prepare two fully competitive cars, so when team manager Peter Warr wanted to bring in British driver Derek Warwick as successor to Elio de Angelis, Ayrton saw this simply as unwarranted aggravation. Warwick was to be signed as number two driver, but Ayrton felt his ambition might be thwarted if he had to deal with the highly motivated Englishman, and vetoed his inclusion in the team in favour of the less experienced Johnny Dumfries. It was another example of Ayrton's incredible honesty, no matter how uncomfortable his decisions might make others.

Ironically, once he had established himself as an absolutely consistent race-winner and number one performer, he had no reservations about going to McLaren and handling Alain Prost in a straight fight. 'All I ask for is equal equipment', he would say. 'I can do the rest.' And of course he could.

- 1986 -

It wasn't just racing talent which suffused Senna's soul, but also a shrewd ability to read the way a race unfolded. Above all, he had a confidence which manifested itself in a degree of intolerance towards other people's viewpoints. This was perhaps merely reflective of such an overwhelming self-belief that he just couldn't grasp that other people might have views which were at variance with his own. For an intelligent man, this was a curious blind spot.

In 1986 Senna won the Spanish and Detroit Grands Prix, both brilliantly opportunistic successes, at the wheel of the superb Lotus-Renault 98T. The former was the first such race to be held at the twisting new track at Jerez de la Frontera and, in historical terms, has gone down as a race which was almost won by Nigel Mansell's Williams-Honda FW11. After a late race stop for fresh tyres, the gallant Englishman apparently slashed into Senna's remaining advantage to pass the chequered flag virtually level with the Brazilian's Lotus.

After the race, Mansell remarked that it was ironic that the start/finish line had been repositioned closer to the final corner. Had it been at its original site, a few metres further down the circuit, he claimed that he would have won. However, the Senna fans preferred to view the race's outcome from the opposite standpoint.

Their interpretation of the situation was that Ayrton had everything perfectly weighed up and was letting out the rope as much as he dared, thereby conserving both his fuel and tyres in the closing moments of the race. It was the closest Grand Prix finish on record, with Senna ahead by one-hundredth of a second. In Ayrton's view, that was all you needed to know.

Ayrton's second win of the 1986 season came on the equally tricky Detroit street circuit, where, despite an early stop to change a punctured tyre, he judged things perfectly to pull off a memorable victory. The latest Lotus 98T was undeniably competitive, and the team started the year confident that they could give their man a realistic chance of winning the championship. He would be on pole position no fewer than eight times, but with the fuel allowance for each race now cut from 220 to 195 litres, the need to balance economy with performance fell into even sharper perspective.

Desperate to keep up with the Honda-propelled Williams in the closing stages of the race, Renault produced some new Garrett turbochargers for their V6 engine and flew them down to Estoril for the Portuguese GP towards the end of the year. Senna duly took pole, but if the Renault engineers were expecting effusive praise, they were to be disappointed.

Renault chief engineer Bernard Dudot recalled: 'All Ayrton said was that if he'd known before what we'd put on the engine, he would have driven his qualifying lap differently.' He wasn't meaning to be ungracious. He was just so totally immersed in his own job that he naturally assumed that everybody else involved in the programme would offer corresponding levels of commitment as a matter of course. That's what we call total commitment!

ANDRETTIS STAR AT INDY 500

Marco Andretti, the nineteen-year-old grandson of US motor racing legend Mario Andretti, came within half a car's length of making motor racing history in 2006 when he was just beaten to a first-time victory in the Indianapolis 500.

Andretti, whose grandfather won the Memorial Day classic in 1969 and went on to win the 1978 F1 world championship, led out onto the final straight in his Dallara-Honda, only for the similar car driven by Sam Hornish Jr to surge past virtually on the finishing line.

Completing the family affair, Michael Andretti, Marco's father, finished a close third in another Dallara-Honda just ahead of Britain's Dan Wheldon, the reigning Indy Racing League champion and winner of the previous year's race.

'I knew I had the car to win, like I knew I was quicker than Dad, actually', said Andretti. 'But [Hornish] just had that speed. I don't know where it came from.'

SO F1 IS A DIFFICULT BUSINESS

These are the eleven teams who currently compete:

Ferrari, Renault, McLaren, Honda, Williams, Red Bull, Toro Rosso, BMW-Sauber, Toyota, Spyker (formerly Midland) and Super Aguri.

These are the 108 teams who have fallen by the wayside since the world championship was inaugurated:

AFM, AGS, ATS, ATS (different), Alfa Romeo, Alta, Amon, Andrea-Moda, Arrows, Aston-Butterworth, Aston-Martin, Apollon, BAR, BRM, BRP, Bellasi, Boro, Brabham, Bugatti, Cisitalia, Coloni, Connaught, Connew, Cooper, Dallara, de Tomaso, Derrington-Francis, EMW, ENB, ERA, Eagle, Emeryson, Ensign, Euro Brun, Ferguson, Fittipaldi, Fondmetal, Footwork, Forti, Frazer-Nash, Fry, Gilby, Gordini, HWM, Hesketh, Hill, JBW, Jaguar, Jordan, Kauhsen, Klenk-Meteor, Kojima, LDS, Lamborghini, Lancia, Larrousse, Lec, Leyton House, Life, Ligier, Lola, Lotus, Lyncar, Maki, March, Martini, Maserati, Matra, McGuire, Mercedes, Merzario, Milano, Minardi, Onyx, Osca, Osella, Pacific, Parnelli, Penske, Porsche, Prost, RAM, Rebaque, Rial, Sauber, Scarab, Schroeder, Scirocco, Shadow, Shannon, Simca-Gordini, Simtek, Spirit, Stebro, Stewart, Surtees, Talbot-Lago, Tec-Mec, Tecno Theodore, Token, Toleman, Trojan, Tyrrell, Vanwall, Veritas, Wolf, Zakspeed.

LAUDA AND PYTHON

Niki Lauda still recalls how he was tutored in a zany British sense of humour during his freshman 1971 season with the works March F2 team contesting the closely-fought European Championship. This was the heyday of *Monty Python's Flying Circus*, and team manager Peter Briggs and all the March mechanics used to breeze about the paddock shouting to each other, as a matter of course, 'albatross', or 'gannet on a stick' and 'this ice cream is bleedin' seabird flavour'.

Lauda and his then fiancée, the serenely beautiful brewery heiress Mariella Reininghaus, thought quite clearly that we were all barking mad, but politely entered into the spirit of it all with great good humour.

Niki's team-mate Ronnie Peterson continued to refer to me as 'Albatross' from that season onwards for the rest of his life. Huge fun!

Off-the-wall
Nicknames for F1 People

Max Mosley was named 'The Great Chicken of Bicester' by an irreverent James Hunt during the early 1970s when the future FIA president ran the March racing team from a base in that Oxfordshire town. Hunt later amended it to 'Le Grand Poulet de Bicester', presumably in a moment of cosmopolitan charm.

Bernie Ecclestone has been nicknamed 'The Bolt' after the long-past UK television programme *The Golden Shot*, presented by Bob Monkhouse in the 1960s. It featured contestants firing a bolt from a crossbow in a contest to split an apple. Monkhouse's assistant Bernie then replaced the ammunition to the accompaniment of the command: 'Bernie, the bolt!' Thus was a legend born.

Niki Lauda was a buck-toothed Austrian kid when he first appeared in an F2 March back in 1971. It was inevitable that he should be nicknamed 'The Mouse', after which, as F1 success beckoned, it was upgraded by general

Niki Lauda

consensus to 'Super Mouse', then to 'Super Rat', and on via 'King Rat' to its ultimate form — just 'The Rat'.

James Hunt — almost inevitably — became 'Hunt the Shunt' after leaving a trail of wrecked F3 cars littered across Europe during the early years of his career.

Ken Tyrrell, the legendary F1 team chief for whom Jackie Stewart won three world championships, was inevitably bestowed with the sobriquet 'Chopper' as his team was originally run from the yard which housed the family timber business.

Jo Siffert, the highly popular Swiss driver who was killed in 1971 when his BRM crashed at Brands Hatch, was always called 'Seppi', a nickname from his childhood in Switzerland.

Gruff New Zealander **Denny Hulme**, who won the world championship in 1967, was — perhaps inevitably — known as 'The Bear'.

James Hunt was partnered by the genial **Jochen Mass** at McLaren in 1976. It didn't take James long to christen him 'Hermann the German', and the name stuck for the balance of his career.

FITTIPALDIS RULE AT HOME

São Paolo's fabled first F1 son Emerson Fittipaldi was 25 years and ten months old when he sped to victory in the 1972 Italian Grand Prix, thereby becoming the youngest competitor to take the title crown. With that in mind, there is a certain strange symmetry to the fact that Fernando Alonso, just 24 years and two months old, would eventually deprive Emmo of that singular distinction by finishing third in the 2005 Brazilian Grand Prix at Interlagos, the track which, during the 1970s, was regarded as the Fittipaldi family's personal backyard.

In the halcyon days of Brazil's international motor racing ascendancy, the Fittipaldis ruled Interlagos as their own private fiefdom. Emerson and his elder brother Wilson were the stars of just about every show in the early 1970s and when they returned to Brazil for the Formula 2 Torneio series, the grandstands were literally heaving at the seams. Under the circumstances, giving Wilson leeway when it came to the strict application of the rules all seemed like part of the fun.

Prior to the start of one race here, Wilson brought his March 712 to the grid and didn't turn his engine off, as he had a battery problem which would preclude the car restarting without a push-start, which in turn would have incurred a penalty.

Keith Leighton, Ronnie Peterson's mechanic, was so incensed that Wilson was obviously trying to pull a fast one that he just strolled across to the Brazilian's car, put his hand into the cockpit and flicked off the ignition switch. Wilson popped his belts and erupted from the cockpit to try to throttle the hapless Leighton, who understandably made himself scarce. But the seething Wilson had to take the penalty.

Of course, I wouldn't want anybody to run away with the idea that the Fittipaldis had special treatment from the stewards in those dim and distant days. In 1976, pole position man James Hunt confessed to being somewhat startled as Carlos Pace's Brabham-Alfa — which had qualified on row three — pulled level with him even before the starter had raised, let alone dropped, the starting flag. All the guys behind said they simply waited until Pace's rear tyres began to spin and then just dropped their clutches and followed. Penalty? Do me a favour.

A FEW MORE FACTS AND STATISTICS

NUMBER OF WORLD CHAMPIONSHIPS SCORED BY AN INDIVIDUAL DRIVER:

- SEVEN -

Michael Schumacher (1994, 1995, 2000–04)

- FIVE -

Juan Manuel Fangio (1951, 1954, 1955, 1956, 1957)

- FOUR -

Alain Prost (1985, 1986, 1989, 1993)

- THREE -

Jack Brabham (1959, 1960, 1966); Jackie Stewart (1969, 1971, 1973); Niki Lauda (1975, 1977, 1984); Nelson Piquet (1981, 1983, 1987); Ayrton Senna (1988, 1990, 1991)

- TWO -

Alberto Ascari (1952, 1953); Graham Hill (1962, 1968); Jim Clark (1963, 1965); Emerson Fittipaldi (1972, 1974); Mika Hakkinen (1998, 1999); Fernando Alonso (2005, 2006)

- ONE -

Giuseppe Farina (1950); Mike Hawthorn (1958); Phil Hill (1961); John Surtees (1964); Denny Hulme (1967); Jochen Rindt (1970); James Hunt (1976); Mario Andretti (1978); Jody Scheckter (1979); Alan Jones (1980); Keke Rosberg (1982); Nigel Mansell (1992); Damon Hill (1996); Jacques Villeneuve (1997).

NUMBER OF POLE POSITIONS PER DRIVER:

68 Michael Schumacher

65 Ayrton Senna

33 Jim Clark, Alain Prost

32 Nigel Mansell

28 Juan Manuel Fangio

26 Mika Hakkinen

24 Niki Lauda, Nelson Piquet

20 Damon Hill

18 Mario Andretti, René Arnoux

17 Jackie Stewart

16 Stirling Moss

15 Fernando Alonso

14 Alberto Ascari, James Hunt, Ronnie Peterson

13 Rubens Barrichello, Jack Brabham, Graham Hill, Jacky Ickx, Juan Pablo Montoya, Jacques Villeneuve

12 Gerhard Berger, David Coulthard

11 Kimi Raikkonen

10 Jochen Rindt

8 Riccardo Patrese, John Surtees

7 Jacques Laffite

6 Emerson Fittipaldi, Phil Hill, Jean-Pierre Jabouille, Alan Jones, Carlos Reutemann, Ralf Schumacher

5 Chris Amon, Giuseppe Farina, Clay Regazzoni, Keke Rosberg, Patrick Tambay

4 Mike Hawthorn, Didier Pironi

3 Tony Brooks, Elio de Angelis, Teo Fabi, Froilan Gonzalez, Dan Gurney, Jean-Pierre Jarier, Jody Scheckter, Jarno Trulli, Felipe Massa, Giancarlo Fisichella, Jenson Button

2 Michele Alboreto, Jean Alesi, Heinz-Harald Frentzen, Stuart Lewis-Evans, Jo Siffert, Gilles Villeneuve, John Watson

1 Lorenzo Bandini, Jo Bonnier, Thierry Boutsen, Vittorio Brambilla, Eugenio Castellotti, Peter Collins, Andrea de Cesaris, Patrick Depailler, Nick Heidfeld, Denny Hulme, Carlos Pace, Mike Parkes, Tom Pryce, Peter Revson, Wolfgang von Trips

Championship Points Scoring

Ever since the official world championship was inaugurated in 1950, the points scoring system whereby the title holder was eventually determined has been the focal point of much controversy and debate. Should it reward consistency? Or should there be a premium benefit placed on winning races, which is what — after all — basically motivates the competitor from the very start?

How they scored:

1950–59:	8-6-4-3-2 for the top five race finishers, plus 1 point for the fastest lap
1960:	8-6-4-3-2-1 for the top six race finishers
1961–90:	9-6-4-3-2-1 for the top six race finishers
1991–2002:	10-6-4-3-2-1 for the top six race finishers
2003 to date:	10-8-6-5-4-3-2-1 for the top eight race finishers

Number of races counted for final classification in drivers' world championship:

1950: .... 4 out of 7
1951: .... 4 out of 8
1952: .... 4 out of 8
1953: .... 4 out of 9
1954: .... 5 out of 9
1955: .... 5 out of 7
1956: .... 5 out of 8
1957: .... 5 out of 8
1958: .... 6 out of 11
1959: .... 5 out of 9
1960: .... 6 out of 10
1961: .... 5 out of 8
1962: .... 5 out of 9
1963: .... 6 out of 10
1964: .... 6 out of 10
1965: .... 6 out of 10
1966: .... 5 out of 9
1967: .... 9 out of 11
1968: .... 10 out of 12
1969: .... 9 out of 11
1970: .... 11 out of 13
1971: .... 9 out of 11
1972: .... 10 out of 12
1973: .... 13 out of 15

1974: .... 13 out of 15
1975: .... 12 out of 14
1976: .... 14 out of 16
1977: .... 15 out of 16
1978: .... 14 out of 16
1979: .... 8 out of 15
1980: ...... 10 out of 14
1981: .... 11 out of 15
1982: .... 11 out of 16
1983: .... 11 out of 15
1984: .... 11 out of 16
1985: .... 11 out of 16
1986: .... 11 out of 16
1987: .... 11 out of 16
1988: .... 11 out of 16
1989: .... 11 out of 16
1990: .... 11 out of 16
1991: .... 16 out of 16
1992: .... 16 out of 16
1993: .... 16 out of 16
1994: .... 16 out of 16
1995: .... 17 out of 17
1996: .... 16 out of 16
1997: .... 17 out of 17
1998: .... 16 out of 16
1999: .... 16 out of 16
2000: ...... 16 out of 16

2001: .... 17 out of 17
2002: ...... 17 out of 17
2003: ...... 16 out of 16
2004: ...... 18 out of 18
2005: ...... 19 out of 19
2006: ...... 18 out of 18

YEARS WHEN THE CHAMPION DID NOT WIN MOST OF THE RACES:

1950: **Farina**, 3 wins = Fangio, 3 wins

1958: **Hawthorn**, 1 win; Moss, 4 wins; Brooks, 3 wins

1959: **Brabham**, 2 wins = Moss, 2 wins = Brooks, 2 wins

1961: **P. Hill**, 2 wins = von Trips, 2 wins = Moss, 2 wins

1964: **Surtees**, 2 wins = Hill, 2 wins; Gurney, 2 wins; Clark, 3 wins

1967: **Hulme**, 2 wins; Clark, 4 wins

1968: **Hill**, 3 wins = Stewart, 3 wins

1974: **Fittipaldi**, 3 wins = Reutemann, 3 wins

1977: **Lauda**, 3 wins; Andretti, 4 wins

1979: **Scheckter**, 3 wins = G. Villeneuve, 3 wins; Jones, 4 wins

1982: **Rosberg**, 1 win; Prost, 2 wins; Watson, 2 wins; Lauda, 2 wins; Arnoux, 2 wins

1983: **Piquet**, 3 wins; Prost, 4 wins

1984: **Lauda**, 5 wins; Prost, 7 wins

1986: **Prost**, 4 wins; Mansell, 5 wins

1987: **Piquet**, 3 wins; Mansell, 4 wins

1989: **Prost**, 3 wins; Senna, 6 wins

What Would Basil Fawlty Have Made of it?

One of the lesser documented episodes of the great good humour which existed between Britain's James Hunt and Austria's Niki Lauda during their epic battle for the 1976 world championship came on the morning of that year's Canadian GP at the Mosport Park circuit near Toronto.

They were occupying adjacent hotel rooms and, just before they left for the track, Niki suddenly came goose-stepping into

James's room, completely togged up in over-alls, helmet and balaclava. 'Today I shall vin zee vorld championship', he announced, before turning on his heel and goose-stepping out again.

But he didn't, of course. Hunt kept the contest wide open until the final race of the year in Japan, where he beat the Austrian by a single point.

SORTING IT OUT ON THE GOLF COURSE

Max Mosley, the future FIA president, and Jackie Stewart first crossed each other's paths at the end of the 1969 season when the Tyrrell team was facing a dilemma. Matra wanted Tyrrell to use its own V12 engine rather than the Ford Cosworth V8 which had powered Stewart to his title the previous year. Neither Tyrrell nor Stewart were interested.

Ironically, it was Mosley who came to the rescue. Together with fellow racers Robin Herd, Alan Rees and Graham Coaker, he had just founded the March company which planned to build its own F1 cars for the following season.

It seemed like an absurd pipe dream at the time, but Mosley was a thrustingly ambitious young man and succeeded in selling a couple of March 701s to Tyrrell for Stewart and his team-mate Johnny Servoz-Gavin to drive in 1970.

Yet even before Stewart first drove the March for the first time in a race, he knew it was a disaster. 'The problems were inherent in the car's design', he said. 'Not the sort of things you can overcome through tuning. The irony was almost funny; the reigning world champion forced by circumstances to suffer with an uncompetitive car.'

In the middle of the season, Ken Tyrrell ditched the March and unveiled his own car which had been developed in secret in less than five months. It wasn't a move which did much for the credibility of Mosley's company at a crucial moment in its development.

A few months later, on the eve of the Canadian GP, Stewart was playing golf with Mosley's business partner Robin Herd, who suggested that if Jackie lost the game, he should drive the March in the following day's race.

'Robin, never has anybody had such an

incentive not to lose a golf match', replied the Scot. Jackie finished one up and raced the Tyrrell.

THE ARISTOCRAT OF
ALL ARISTOCRATS

Probably the most aristocratic and well connected of the 1950s motor racing playboys was the Marquis de Portago, the larger-than-life Spanish nobleman who cast a giant shadow far longer than his modest tally of five Grand Prix outings might perhaps have suggested.

Raised in Biarritz while his father fought for Franco in the Spanish Civil War, 'Fon' shared the second place Lancia-Ferrari with Peter Collins in the 1956 British GP at Silverstone. But he was also an all-round sportsman of dazzling versatility, twice riding in the Grand National as well as being a member of Spain's Olympic bobsleigh team. He and his wife lived in some style in a mansion on the exclusive Avenue Foch in Paris and numbered the Duke and Duchess of Windsor among their regular dinner guests.

Portago was born in London. At the age of

seventeen he held a pilot's licence in America, but had it almost immediately suspended after an incident when, for a $500 bet, he flew under a bridge which had barely enough clearance for the wings. 'The authorities were only upset because one of its wheels touched the water', he offered by way of explanation.

Fon de Portago was killed at the wheel of his works Ferrari sports car, together with his co-driver and long-time friend Ed Nelson and a group of spectators, in the 1957 Mille Miglia road race, a disaster which led to the permanent cancellation of this historic event. It was yet another reminder that Fon's generation of FI drivers lived in an era when, although sex was still safe, motor racing remained uncompromisingly and relentlessly dangerous.

CLIFF ALLISON:
WHERE'S MY PRIVATE JET?

Cliff Allison was a member of that elite band of British racing drivers to be recruited by the Ferrari FI team, but unlike such celebrities as Mike Hawthorn, Tony Brooks, John Surtees and Nigel Mansell, his career with the famous Italian squad passed without a single Grand Prix victory and was certainly one of the briefest, amounting to just six races.

His best result in a Ferrari was second place in the by-now-dated front-engined Dino 246, behind Bruce McLaren's mid-engined Cooper, in the 1960 Argentine Grand Prix at Buenos Aires. Yet within another few months Allison, who died aged 73 in April 2005, was involved in a huge accident practising for the Monaco Grand Prix which effectively finished his top line career for good. 'I woke up in hospital speaking French, which was strange because I didn't know any French', he would recount.

A farmer whose family also owned the local garage business, Allison was born and lived all his life in Brough, a windswept village in Cumbria. At the age of twenty he drove his first race at the now-defunct Charterhall track in Scotland at the wheel of his own 500cc Formula 3 Cooper, and he stayed competing in this category until 1956, by which time he had successfully made his name as a man to watch.

In 1957 he shared a Lotus Eleven sports

car with Keith Hall at Le Mans and finished an impressive 14th overall in this tiny 744cc-engined machine, winning the prestigious Index of Performance handicap in the process. Allison's speed convinced Lotus team owner Colin Chapman to give him a drive in Formula 1 alongside Graham Hill in 1957, which in turn led to the invitation to sign for Ferrari in '59.

Today, Ferrari F1 drivers are multi-millionaire international sportsmen criss-crossing Europe in a couple of hours aboard their private jets. Allison raced at a time when they were meagrely rewarded, and he recounted how he made the gruelling trip from Cumbria to Maranello on a fortnightly basis. 'Oh it wasn't really any problem', he said with a grin. 'I used to drive to Darlington, get the express train to Kings Cross, taxi to Cromwell Road air terminal, bus to Heathrow, plane to Milan, taxi to the station, train to Modena and taxi out to the Ferrari factory at Maranello.'

Simple really.

INNES SHOULD HAVE
STAYED IN THE BAR

Many people find it almost impossible to believe the high spirits and wildly extrovert behaviour which characterised much of the off-track behaviour among the drivers in the 1950s and 60s.

Foremost among the hell-raisers in the early 1960s was Innes Ireland. The hard-driving, hard-drinking son of a vet from Kirkcudbright, Ireland was probably too sociable a personality to make the most of his considerable natural talent. Driving for Colin Chapman's Team Lotus, Innes produced some brilliant performances, most notably his victory in the 1961 US GP at the Watkins Glen track in upstate New York, and his similarly memorable win over the Porsche team in the non-championship road race on the magnificent Solitude circuit near Stuttgart.

After his win at Solitude, or so the story goes, Innes got so plastered that he ended up on the roof of a local hotel, firing a loaded pistol into the air, bursting open the hotel bar after it had closed and then lamping 'mein host' when he attempted to calm everybody down again. As a result of all this horseplay, the organisers of the German GP at the Nürburgring — due to be run a fortnight after the Solitude fixture — announced that they weren't going to allow him to compete. In the end, of course, the whole episode was forgotten and Innes was allowed to take part.

REMEMBERING RONNIE

A personal memoir about the charismatic Swedish driver who died from his injuries after crashing his Lotus 78 at the start of the 1978 Italian Grand Prix at Monza.

It was an era when the world seemed young and our horizons limitless. The 1971 European Formula 2 championship was one of the closest-fought motor racing series which I ever experienced. It shaped my formative years as a motor racing journalist and cemented my friendship with Ronnie Peterson.

So how do I recall Ronnie, and what was he like? Well, this tall blond Swede who I first rode with in the passenger seat of his Mercedes 250 saloon around the soaking Pau road circuit in south-west France was a uniquely charismatic soul. He blended the easy manner of Mika Hakkinen with the driving genius of Kimi Raikkonen and the light-hearted impishness of Stefan Johansson. Add to that the fact that he was joined in the F2 paddock by the likes of Niki Lauda, Emerson Fittipaldi, François Cevert and Tim Schenken, and you can see why I found the '71 season such a magical experience.

Ronnie was straightforward and delightfully uncomplicated. His sheer speed at the wheel of that March 712M was baffling to behold. There were several such cars contesting the championship, but Ronnie wrapped his around his little finger like a go-kart. It literally danced around the circuits of Europe, carrying its intrepid young driver to his great successes as an aspiring star.

There was a great sense of community in those days. We ate together, often travelled together, and there was a wonderful feeling that we were all growing up together, that we would one day be in F1, and that eventually proved to be the case, although I reached it as a journalist two years after Ronnie did as a driver. While he was on his way to winning the

1971 European F2 championship he was also busy driving the works March 711 in world championship Grands Prix on alternate weekends. Five times he would finish second, and he ended up runner-up to Jackie Stewart in the final points table.

He was incredibly loyal to the March team, and that was much appreciated by its directors Max Mosley and Robin Herd – even in the face of Colin Chapman's efforts to poach him to drive for Lotus. Chapman tried it on at the end of 1971, but Ronnie was happy to stay with the team which had originally given him his chance in the F1 front line, and would not move to Lotus until his contract expired at the end of 1972.

'He was the only driver I ever met who appreciated the risk we were taking in offering him a three-year contract', recalled Mosley. 'We paid him £2,000 in 1970, £5,000 in 1971 and £10,000 in 1972. He was totally loyal and would never have dreamed of breaking that commitment.'

Fast though he undeniably was in the March, it wasn't until he got in the Lotus 72 in 1973 that SuperSwede, as we knew him, finally caught his stride and had the equipment beneath him to prove he was the fastest man in the F1 business. Although in 1976 he would move back to March for a second stint with the team, in 1978 he would rejoin Lotus for another assault on the world championship. But, tragically, we all know how that ended.

On the morning of 10 September 1978, I stopped to chat with Ronnie in the paddock at Monza. To this day I can remember the very spot. He was dressed in those trademark yellow overalls and sunglasses. We talked for a couple of minutes, no more. It was the last time I ever saw this fine man and I miss him still.

JAMES HUNT: THE MOTOR RACING MAVERICK

I may have imagined James Hunt throwing an empty Chivas Regal whisky bottle out of an 18th-floor window of São Paolo's Othon Palace Hotel in the autumn of 1972 when we were all out in Brazil for the Torneio winter F2 series, but I don't think that I did.

Hell, James wouldn't be driving in F1 for another six months — and wouldn't win the world championship with McLaren for another four years — but he was already being tutored in the sport's wilder side by Mike Hailwood. Between them, their insatiable appetite for the gentler sex decimated even the admittedly frisky — and unimaginably beautiful — immediate post-teenage female community of that pulsating Brazilian city. In fact, many of us returned from that trip more seasoned in the ways of the world than we may have originally anticipated as we departed on the outward leg of our journey as strangely uneasy innocents abroad.

James was also a great golfing fan and on that Brazilian odyssey struck up a friendship with a sprightly octogenarian American expatriate, alongside whom he pounded up the fairways at a particularly exclusive local country club.

H. Barney Gengenbach had come out to Brazil in the early years of the century, as I understood it, to help develop the railway network. He also drove a Triumph TR4 which, even in 1972, must have been the least suitable car on earth for the rutted, 'three ply' roads of São Paolo. Nevertheless, he was enormously hospitable, and had a Lebanese wife, and we found ourselves invited to an afternoon tea party that appeared to be the São Paolo chapter of the Lebanese Expatriates' Association.

'Come on Hens, rally the troops, we've got to be on parade for Barney and his missus', said James inspirationally. So we did just that, and dutifully turned out to be pleasant and sociable, clinking tea cups with the likes of James, Hailwood and Ian Phillips — later to become commercial director of the Jordan F1 team, but then a disreputable journo like myself — amid the unlikely setting of the blue rinse brigade in that South American city.

Back in London a couple of months later, I was sleeping comfortably on a mattress on the lounge floor of the west London flat of a mutual friend when suddenly the lights clicked on at about 4 am. Rubbing my eyes, I discerned an apologetic James in the company of a winsome and slightly embarrassed young girl whom I also recognised.

'Sorry 'bout this, Hens', said James with great charm. 'Need the bed. You know how it is!'

I was at least permitted to keep my duvet, and curled up in the hall while James took his pleasure.

Some years later I took my young family to the British Grand Prix for the first time, where James met them. 'Ah', he said warmly, 'so these are the Henlets'. James's charisma was all-embracing in the way it crossed generational boundaries. His sudden death in 1993 — from a heart attack at just 45 — ambushed all our emotions. Even now, when the phone rings, I half expect to hear his cheery voice: 'Hello, Hens. J. Hunt here ...'

THE DAY HESKETH BEAT FERRARI

Thirty-two years ago Hesketh beat Ferrari. This is an abridged version of a feature I wrote for *F1 Racing* magazine in 2005:

> Ask Niki Lauda about James Hunt and their battles together back in the 1970s and his face will crinkle into an untypical grin and he'll almost gurgle with pleasure. James was one of his mates. Not sleekly polished F1-style mate, you understand, but band-of-brothers, scurfing around together in F2, coming up the hard way mate. OK, so James didn't have the dosh enjoyed by the Lauda banking dynasty, but both had to make their way in the F1 business because

James Hunt

their disapproving parents didn't give them a cent.

By the summer of '75, they were both F1 front runners. Niki, shrewdly and reflecting his ascetic, calculating character, had secured himself a berth at Ferrari. James, meanwhile, had hitched his star to Lord Hesketh's wagon to establish a reputation as F1's playboy prince. Yet that was only a superficial image. The portly peer may have occasionally quaffed champagne as if it were Red Bull, but primarily he wanted to cock a snook at the F1 establishment. And that meant he wanted James to win.

Hesketh's great day came at Zandvoort in the '75 Dutch Grand Prix. Thanks to some clever strategy on the wind-blown seaside circuit through the sand dunes near Amsterdam, James held off Niki to score his first Grand Prix win by one-tenth of a second.

'What you've got to understand about my relationship with James is that it was based on a lot of mutual respect built up over the previous four years,' said Niki reflectively. 'I'd first met him in 1971 when I'd come to England to drive for the semi-works March F2 team. I really didn't know too many people and I rented a studio flat from Max Mosley just around the back of Victoria Station.

'By the start of 1975 I was settled in at Ferrari. We'd got the new 312T on stream, equipped with the new transverse gearbox which improved the chassis balance compared to the previous year's B3 which I'd used to post a fairly easy win at Zandvoort, although the weather was fine that day, not like the weather which we experienced in 1975 which was cool and a bit depressing from memory.

'To be honest, I knew James and the Hesketh 308 couldn't be ignored, but up to Zandvoort they hadn't really developed the consistency needed to win. But I knew they were quick enough. In the non-championship F1 race at Silverstone earlier in the year I'd sat behind James who led the race until his engine broke. I went on to beat Emerson Fittipaldi's McLaren at the end, but I knew James had the speed.

'I'm really not good on remembering all the day-to-day detail of the races in which I competed, but I've got quite a clear recollection of this race at Zandvoort. I do remember qualifying on pole, but I'd have to take your word that I was looking a bit on the worried side before the start because the

Ferrari team had opted for an engine change in my car the night before the race.

'Before the start the track was wet and I obviously started on rain tyres. James took the pretty brave decision to come in for dry weather tyres on lap seven. That dropped him from fourth to 19th place from memory, which you might think wrote him out of contention, but was in fact something of a strategic master stroke. You see James had opted for a full dry set-up on his Hesketh which meant that the track conditions really started to come to him as the circuit dried out. I stayed out in the lead to the end of lap 13, which was probably a lap too long when you consider that as I accelerated back out of the pits James was coming past at full speed and was able to get ahead of my Ferrari as we went into Tarzan, that tricky 180-degree right hander at the end of the start-finish straight.

'I remember thinking "dammit, that's screwed things" because I'd set up my car with something of a compromise for the wet and dry conditions. Now I was slightly on the back foot, so there was nothing left for me to do but keep the pressure on as best I could all the way to the finish. I figured that if I could really rattle him he might make a small mistake, in which case I'd be through and away into the lead. Perhaps I could wrong-foot him in slower traffic. But no way. Despite the fact that I'd got the nose of my Ferrari right under the rear wing of his Hesketh from time to time, he wouldn't give me an inch. After 75 laps of this I was just over a second behind.

'No doubt about it, James drove beautifully and there was, quite understandably, a great deal of excitement amongst the British press about his achievement, even though, to be totally honest, I kept a bit in hand as my main priority was to score championship points that day. But that win took James through a psychological barrier which I would learn about to my cost when he moved to McLaren in 1975.

'As far as the celebrations in the Hesketh pit were concerned I can recall a lot of champagne being sprayed about the place, which was understandable, but I really don't remember James giving everybody the finger. I remember that I stood on the rostrum holding up six fingers, indicating the number of points I'd just won for second place. I'd like to have won myself, of course, but James wasn't ready to be beaten that day and really deserved his big moment.'

What Happened Next?

James Hunt joined McLaren in 1976 and beat his old pal Lauda to the world championship by a single point, even though Niki missed three races after his fiery Ferrari shunt at the Nürburgring. He would stay with McLaren through to the end of 1978, briefly switching to the Wolf team the following year before abruptly retiring mid-season, his fear of death and injury overwhelming his motivation.

After his retirement, Hunt made a successful name for himself by carving out a niche as BBC's F1 expert, working alongside the legendary Murray Walker. He died at his home in Wimbledon from a heart attack over the weekend of the Canadian GP in June 1993.

Niki Lauda regained his championship crown for Ferrari in 1977 and retired from driving two years later to concentrate on his new airline, Lauda Air. Financially strapped, he returned to racing with McLaren from 1982–85 before retiring for good. Today he is an F1 television commentator for RTL between piloting an Airbus for his new budget airline Niki.

Alexander Hesketh went on to become president of the British Racing Drivers' Club and Conservative Chief Whip in the House of Lords. In 2004 he put his family seat, Easton Neston, near Towcester — scene of some wild parties in the Hesketh Racing days — on the market for £50m.

Bubbles Horsley stayed on with Hesketh to the end of 1977, running cars for diverse drivers including Harald Ertl, Rupert Keegan and Ian Ashley before quitting his involvement with the sport to concentrate his focus on property development.

Harvey Postlethwaite — the Hesketh designer — followed Hunt to the Wolf team in 1979 before gaining the prestigious appointment of Ferrari technical director in 1981, where he stayed until 1990. Then he moved to Tyrrell, back to Ferrari in 1992, and then to Tyrrell again in 1993. After Tyrrell was swallowed up by BAR in 1998, Harvey took over command of the emergent Honda F1 programme, which was scrapped in 1999 after Harvey's death from a heart attack in Barcelona while attending an April test session at the Circuit de Catalunya.

The Girls Who Keep Us Happy

The emancipation of women in the F1 business has been a long time coming. Many outsiders still regard the sport as one of the last bastions of male chauvinism, but over the last three decades that perception may have changed significantly.

Back in the 1960s it was only drivers' wives or girlfriends who were involved on the fringes of the action, a stopwatch thrust into their hands with the instruction to start recording their other half's laps in those dark ages before electronic timing systems.

Yet it was probably the arrival of 'PR and marketing' in the mid-1980s which really accelerated the promotion of F1's female generation, the Williams team's PR Ann Bradshaw for a while gathering quite a cult following among those courtesy coach drivers serving the long-term car parks at Heathrow. She was almost better known than the drivers. All of which tells you a lot about F1 earning power. These days you're as likely to see an F1 driver in an airport car park as you are Ron Dennis on a Circle Line tube.

Following in Annie B's wake came the current crop of highly efficient and attractive ladies to whom we all defer admiringly in the F1 media centres across the world: Ellen Kolby (McLaren), Tracy Novak (Honda), Silvia Hoffer (Williams), Stefania Bocci (Ferrari), Katie Tweedle (Red Bull), Fabiana Valenti (Toro Rosso), Emma Bearpark (Super Aguri), Fernanda Vilas (Toyota) and Charlotte Anderson (Spyker, formerly Midland). Annie herself is back on her old beat now, working for the BMW-Sauber squad. Oh yes, and just in case I'm accused of reverse discrimination, let's not forget the only man at this particular party, Renault F1's equally efficient and obliging Bradley Lord.

OK, so that was the line-up at the end of the 2006 season. It's always dangerous to start making lists like this, so apologies to anybody who feels they've been left out unjustly. However, the onset of corporate schmoozing has opened up a completely fresh area of development in the F1 business, with the result that we pampered hacks are frequently spoiled for choice when it comes to impeccable food served up by gorgeous young ladies.

What's more, working as one of the catering staff in an F1 paddock has to a large extent eclipsed the job of chalet girl on the ski slopes as the ideal choice of gap year employment. The end result, of course, is that the lissom young blonde pouring your glass of chilled Chardonnay at the McLaren communications centre has probably just majored in social psychology or anthropology.

In simple terms, she's a damn sight cleverer than you are.

RON DENNIS:
THE PURSUIT OF PERFECTION

Winning British Grands Prix at Silverstone is nothing new under Ron Dennis's stewardship of the McLaren team. Juan Pablo Montoya's victory at Silverstone in July 2005 was McLaren's tenth British Grand Prix victory since Ron took control of the team during the course of 1980. Eight of those wins were at Silverstone, two at Brands Hatch. Prior to Ron's era, the team had won three times at Silverstone, their first British GP triumph being achieved in 1973 thanks to the efforts of that great American driver Peter Revson.

Today Ron is one of the sport's grandees, a CBE and a vice president of the British Racing Drivers' Club (BRDC). A multi-millionaire who presides over the McLaren Group from its £300m high-tech head-quarters near Woking, his is one of the great success stories of contemporary motor racing history.

Yet he is also admired and respected for his support for Silverstone and the British Grand Prix. Both in the negotiations between the BRDC and the Interpublic Group – as the giant US media company sought to terminate its motor sports involvement last year – and advising on the best way to secure the future of the British Grand Prix, Ron's measured counsel and steady hand have been of huge benefit to the club.

Meet Ron Dennis for the first time and you may gain the initial impression of some-body who is both distant and aloof. Having known him for 35 years, I have long since concluded that this is a mixture of shyness and a reluctance to wear his heart on his sleeve. His private life with his American wife Lisa and their three children is conducted away

from the spotlight of publicity. This in itself
is an attractive quality, but deal with him on
a business footing and he's a formidable
opponent, combining a shrewd ability to
quickly assimilate other people's negotiating
stance with flashes of a sledgehammer lack
of subtlety which can throw you suddenly
off guard.

The late Ken Tyrrell summed up Ron by
saying: 'First of all, Ron is a guy who loves his
motor racing. He really likes his racing. He is
absolutely straightforward and honest. I would
trust him with my life, if that is not too much
of an exaggeration.'

Yet Ron knows from his own personal
experience that it was not always like that,
particularly when he started out on his own
career path 40 years ago. 'It was a bit like
walking round a building with no windows and
only two doors. The only ways in were as a
driver — which meant you had to have private
means — or as a mechanic.' Dennis entered F1
as a mechanic, attending his first Grand Prix
working on Jochen Rindt's Cooper-Maserati
in the summer of 1966. He was just nineteen
years old.

In those days most racing car factories

were dark, dank and oily places. Cooper's base in Surbiton was no exception. Yet even in these early years of his career, Ron always tried to keep himself as smartly dressed and clean as possible, not always an easy task. When you first encounter the spick and span working conditions of today's McLaren Technical Centre, you begin to understand how difficult it must have been for Ron in those formative years.

Dennis stayed with Cooper until the end of 1967 and followed Rindt on his switch to Jack Brabham's team. Rindt, a contemporary and close friend of fellow racer Jackie Stewart, projected an outwardly popular image, but Dennis saw how he treated some of the people he worked with and quickly came to the conclusion that the famous Austrian driver was a bit too big for his boots.

By the end of 1970, Dennis could see that there was no real future working for other people if he seriously wanted to make his own impact on the business of motorsport. Together with his fellow former Brabham mechanic Neil Trundle, he started an independent Formula 2 team at a time when this category was the key feeder series below

F1. Rondel Racing, as it was titled, set the tenor for all Dennis's subsequent achievements. Painstaking care and attention to detail quickly became established as its hallmarks.

Almost a decade later, these were the qualities which Philip Morris, the McLaren F1 team's title sponsor, homed in on when they insisted that the then-struggling organisation amalgamated with Ron's Project Four operation. It really was a case of sink or swim. Once in the organisational driving seat, Dennis began the process of turning the team around, a task which was highlighted by his colleague John Barnard's pioneering work in developing carbon fibre composite chassis technology, possibly the biggest single engineering advance for driver safety in the sport's history.

The rest, as they say, is history. More than two decades later, Dennis continues to attend all the races and has a simple philosophy. 'McLaren exists to win every race in which it competes', he explains. 'Worrying about what your rivals are doing is a fruitless exercise. If you win all the races, or as many as you possibly can, then hopefully the world championship will flow logically from those efforts. I am not a person who looks backwards and worries about what has gone before. The only priority for McLaren is looking ahead and aiming to win the next race.'

Put like that, it seems quite logical, doesn't it?

WHERE THEY HELD THE RACES SINCE THE START OF THE OFFICIAL F1 WORLD CHAMPIONSHIP IN 1950

— ARGENTINE GRAND PRIX —

Buenos Aires: 1953–58, 1960, 1972–75, 1977–81, 1995–98

— AUSTRALIAN GRAND PRIX —

Adelaide: 1985–95

Albert Park (Melbourne): 1996 to date

— AUSTRIAN GRAND PRIX —

Zeltweg: 1964

Osterreichring: 1970–87

A1 Ring: 1997–2003

— Bahrain Grand Prix —

Sakhir: 2004 to date

— Belgian Grand Prix —

Spa-Francorchamps: 1950–56, 1958,
1960–68, 1970, 1983, 1985–2002,
2004–2005

Nivelles: 1972, 1974

Zolder: 1973, 1975–82, 1984

— Brazilian Grand Prix —

Interlagos: 1973–77, 1979, 1980, 1990 to date

Jacarepagua (Rio): 1978, 1981–89

— British Grand Prix —

Silverstone: 1950–54, 1956, 1958, 1960,
1963, 1965, 1967, 1969, 1971, 1973, 1975,
1977, 1979, 1981, 1983, 1985, 1987 to date

Brands Hatch: 1964, 1966, 1968, 1970, 1972,
1974, 1976, 1978, 1980, 1982, 1984, 1986

Aintree: 1955, 1957, 1959, 1961, 1962

— Canadian Grand Prix —

Mosport Park: 1967, 1969, 1971–74, 1976–77

St Jovite: 1968, 1970

Montreal: 1978–86, 1988 to date

— Chinese Grand Prix —

Shanghai: 2004 to date

— Dutch Grand Prix —

Zandvoort: 1952–55, 1958–71, 1973-85

— European Grand Prix —

Brands Hatch: 1983, 1985

Donington Park: 1993

Nürburgring: 1984, 1995-96, 1999 to date

Jerez: 1997

— French Grand Prix —

Reims: 1950, 1951, 1952, 1953, 1954, 1956,
1958, 1959, 1960, 1961, 1963, 1966

Rouen-les-Essarts: 1957, 1962, 1964, 1968

Clermont-Ferrand: 1965, 1969, 1970, 1972

Dijon-Prenois: 1974, 1977, 1979, 1981, 1984

Paul Ricard: 1971, 1973, 1975, 1976, 1978, 1980, 1982, 1983, 1985, 1986, 1987, 1988, 1989, 1990

Magny-Cours 1991 to date

Le Mans Bugatti: 1967

— German Grand Prix —

Nürburgring: 1951–54, 1956–58, 1961–69, 1971–76, 1985

Avus: 1959

Hockenheim: 1970, 1977–84, 1986 to date

— Hungarian Grand Prix —

Hungaroring: 1986 to date

— Italian Grand Prix —

Monza: 1950–79, 1981 to date

Imola: 1980

— Japanese Grand Prix —

Mount Fuji: 1976, 1977

Suzuka: 1987 to date

— Luxembourg Grand Prix —

Nürburgring: 1997, 1998

— Malaysian Grand Prix —

Sepang: 1999 to date

— Mexican Grand Prix —

Mexico City: 1963–70, 1986–91

— Monaco Grand Prix —

Monte Carlo: 1950, 1955 to date.

— Moroccan Grand Prix —

Ain Diab (Casablanca): 1958

— Pacific Grand Prix —

TI Aida: 1994, 1995

— Pescara Grand Prix —

Pescara (Italy): 1957

— Portuguese Grand Prix —

Oporto: 1958, 1960

Montsanto Park: 1959

Estoril: 1984–96

— San Marino Grand Prix —

Imola: 1981 to date

— South African Grand Prix —

East London: 1962–63, 1965

Kyalami: 1967–80, 1982–85, 1992-93

— Spanish Grand Prix —

Pedralbes: 1951, 1954

Jarama: 1968, 1970, 1972, 1974, 1976–81

Montjuich Park: 1969, 1971, 1973, 1975

Jerez: 1986–90

Catalunya: 1991 to date

— Swedish Grand Prix —

Anderstorp: 1973–78

— Swiss Grand Prix —

Bremgarten (Berne): 1950–54

Dijon-Prenois: 1982

— Turkish Grand Prix —

Istanbul Park: 2005, 2006

— United States Grands Prix —
(various titles)

Sebring: 1959

Riverside: 1960

Watkins Glen: 1961–80

Long Beach: 1976–83

Detroit: 1982–88

Dallas: 1984

Phoenix: 1989–90, 1991

Las Vegas: 1981, 1982

Whose Car is it Anyway?
The Arrows/Shadow High
Court Copyright Case of 1978

It was another of those 'why do I open my mouth' moments. Walking into the Shadow team's garage at Silverstone at the start of the 1978 International Trophy meeting, I clapped eyes on their new DN8 challenger for the first time.

'Good Heavens', I blurted. 'It's an Arrows A1.' Except that I didn't say 'Good Heavens'. How could I ever have imagined that, three months later, I would be having those words quoted back to me in the witness box of the High Court in London's Strand? But that's exactly what happened!

After having worked for Don Nichols' Shadow organisation since its F1 debut in 1973, former driver Jackie Oliver, team manager Alan Rees and designer Tony Southgate decided to leave and go it alone. Unfortunately, it seems that Southgate mistakenly believed that the design was his copyright rather than Shadow's, with the result that they all became involved in this extremely embarrassing and well publicised legal confrontation which they inevitably lost.

Flying with the Tyrrells

My friends in the F1 business hold up my fear of flying as one of the most curious facets of my personality, considering the very large proportion of the last 34 years I've spent bucketing about the inky blackness at 35,000 feet in a large aluminium cigar tube.

I think I should clarify the position. It's not *flying* I worry about, but *crashing*. And until somebody comes up with an explanation I can fully understand as to how 350-ton aeroplanes manage to shudder off the runway into the sky, then this will be an ongoing personal dilemma. More to the point, why do British Airways captains always sound laid-back to the point of being horizontal? They always understate the severity of the weather conditions in well-honed Weybridge tones to the point where you almost begin to believe that the turbulence threatening to rip off the starboard wing can be described as 'a bit of bumpiness' or — my favourite expression of all — 'light chop'.

Kenneth Tyrrell — the legendary F1 team boss's elder son — once told me that in a 33-year career flying with BA, which took him from BAC 1-11s through to Boeing 747-400s, he never once had to shut down an aircraft's engine with any sort of a problem. I must say I was pretty impressed with that, although quite why I can't imagine on second thoughts, because that's what he and they were up there for. *Staying* up there, if you catch my drift.

I have to say I'll always remember flying back from the 1997 Argentine GP on a BA 747 captained by Kenneth with his proud parents, Ken and Norah, up in the first class cabin, trusting to their first-born's piloting skills.

It's a long old haul, non-stop from Buenos Aires up to Heathrow — about fourteen hours — and by the end of it you're always poised to sign up that you'll never fly again. But about an hour from our destination, Kenneth put a smile on all our faces.

'This is the captain speaking', he announced modestly. 'Journey's end almost in sight, but a quick personal message to somebody very special on this flight ... Happy birthday, Mum!'

With Niki on the Flight Deck

It was one of the more surreal experiences of my motor racing career. Pounding across northern Iran at 39,000 feet by the light of a full moon on the flight deck of a Lauda Air Boeing 777. I was sitting on the spare seat between the captain — one Andreas-Nikolaus Lauda, former triple F1 world champion — and his impressively composed young First Officer, who probably hadn't anticipated flying with his boss when he signed in at his Vienna base that afternoon. We were en route to the 1999 Australian Grand Prix.

While freely acknowledging that I've never been a fashion plate — or indeed an arbiter of sartorial style — I have to confess that my dear friend Niki all too often looks as though he has dressed in the dark. He reminds me about the old joke: 'The lights have fused just as you walk into a cupboard which has ten pairs of black socks and ten pairs of white socks. How many do you have to rummage around for before you're sure you've got a matching pair?'

The answer, of course, is three (think about it), but somehow The Rat always seemed to stop at two. But on this occasion Captain Lauda was nattily dressed in a polo shirt covered by a sweatshirt, worn jeans and a pair of deck shoes. Oh yes, and the trademark red baseball cap he's worn ever since sustaining those terrible burns at Nürburgring in 1976.

Lauda Air in its original incarnation was a terrific airline, reflecting the attention to detail which had become Niki's hallmark through a long and illustrious racing career. The food was impeccable, the hostesses both gorgeous and efficient. Unfortunately the company was eventually swallowed up by Austrian Airlines, since which time it has been reduced to a subservient sub-brand. Watching an Austrian Airlines girl asking Niki to spell his name when he checked in at Osaka's Kansai airport after a recent Japanese Grand Prix would have been acutely embarrassing if only Niki could have cared less. But he grinned and shared the joke like the rest of us.

Eventually Lauda went off to establish yet another airline, a European budget operation called 'Niki' for which he still pilots regularly on their fleet of Airbus A320s.

I rang him one day on his mobile. 'Bit busy now', he said in clipped tones. 'What the hell's all that noise?' I asked him. 'Just taxiing in at Ciampino [Rome]', he replied. 'Well, you shouldn't be using your mobile', I said. 'I'm the bloody captain, I say what goes', he replied. No answer to that one!

JACKIE STEWART:
MAKING SAFETY SEXY

Jackie made his Grand Prix debut in the 1965 South African GP at East London, driving a BRM V8. He had completed 99 world championship qualifying races by the time he hung up his helmet just over eight years later. He had been three times world champion, and won a then-record 27 Grands Prix. And he had seen no fewer than eight of his colleagues killed in action in those races, as well as experiencing the death of the legendary Jim Clark, a fellow Scot and soulmate, in an F2 race at Hockenheim.

Much water has flowed under the bridge since May 1964, when Jackie and his wife Helen set off from Glasgow to drive to Monaco in an MGB sports car. They stopped to stay with F1 driver Bruce McLaren in

Surbiton. When they got to Dover, they found that their ferry tickets and travellers' cheques had blown off the roof of the car back in rural Surrey as they accelerated away on their journey.

Consequently they had to invest in a pair of one-way air tickets to the Mediterranean principality. Thankfully, they got there with plenty of time for Jackie to win the prestigious Monaco Grand Prix F3 supporting race, a success which launched the 25-year-old Scot on the road to fame, fortune and three world championship crowns.

'We were staying in Rocquebrune, just along the coast, and on the first day we walked into Monaco because I did not have enough money for a taxi', he said. 'But I won the F3 race, which attracted more prize money than third place in the Grand Prix. At the gala dinner I sat alongside Princess Grace — and then drove back to England in a borrowed Ford Zodiac towing an empty trailer.'

The Stewarts never had to walk to Monaco again. From then on, Jackie and Helen would regularly dine at Monaco's royal palace as personal guests of Prince Rainier. He won the fairy-tale race on no fewer than three occasions – 1966, 1971 and 1973.

In 1997 his own team, Stewart Grand Prix, contested the Monaco Grand Prix for the first time, and Rubens Barrichello finished a magnificent second behind Michael Schumacher's Ferrari.

Thirty years earlier, he had watched in horror from the pits as Lorenzo Bandini's Ferrari crashed at the waterfront chicane and exploded in a fireball which left the popular Italian mortally injured. The tragedy strengthened Stewart's determination to crusade for improved motor racing safety, a task which brought him into head-on collision with the sport's traditionalists.

'It was another example of the incredibly poor facilities which existed in motor racing at that time', he said. 'It was a big fire, another demonstration of how inadequate the whole business was in terms of safety. You found yourself becoming an expert at finding those undertakers with the necessary expertise to move bodies from country to country, you found out that some airlines would not carry a coffin in a passenger plane.'

By general consent, Stewart scored one of the very best wins of his career at Monaco in

1971. Despite suffering from a badly upset stomach, he qualified his Tyrrell-Ford on pole position, only to find the brake balance bar broken as he took his place on the grid, leaving him with braking on the front wheels only. Unconcerned, he led from start to finish, then was sick on the winner's rostrum.

With a touch of modesty, he plays down the magnitude of that achievement. 'Although you might not think so, Monaco is not particularly hard on brakes because you are never slowing from really high speed', he said. 'But it was a good race. To do it with only two-wheel braking was quite something. It's also worth remembering that we had manual gearboxes in those days — and that meant a maximum of 2,800 gearchanges during the course of the race with the six-speed box we had on the old BRM. You always ended the race with your gearchange hand badly blistered.'

Stewart resolutely stood out for safety improvements at a time when he was regarded as an eccentric by the dyed-in-the-wool traditionalists who believed that the risk of death or serious injury was all part and parcel of the challenge. How, asked the detractors, could it be worthwhile if there was no danger involved? Surely cheating death was part of the attraction?

No, responded Stewart. Not so. I'm paid to drive and demonstrate my skill. Not to kill myself.

DAMON HILL: LOW-KEY SON OF A FAMOUS FATHER

The son of the twice world champion Graham Hill, who was killed with five others when his Piper Aztec aeroplane crashed in fog on Arkley golf course while trying to land at Elstree in November 1975, Damon and his sisters Bridget and Samantha all grew up as members of the motor racing community.

'Certainly Silverstone has a lot of memories', he recalled. 'We used to fly in with Dad's plane and in those days, having a twin-prop aircraft was a big thing. To fly into the circuit was a traditional day out for us.

'I used to be left in the timing booth over-looking the startline and the entrance to the pits which was the base for the Doghouse Club [an informal association of racing drivers' wives] and a real hell hole for a young kid, to be honest. I also remember trying to listen to Arsenal playing Leeds in the cup final while my father was winning the 1971 International Trophy race.'

He added: 'This is also the place where Dad announced his retirement from racing, and did a lap of honour, just a few months before he was killed. He never won the British Grand Prix despite having some great races, but I managed to win in 1994, which emphasises the fact that this location has strong sentimental ties with our family.

'Sitting outside Frank Williams's motor-home after that win, signing autographs, was certainly a great experience. I can't forget that this was also the track at which I made my Formula 1 debut in 1992, where I took the chequered flag just behind Nigel Mansell's winning Williams, although four laps behind him.'

British Grand Prix RIP?

This is the text of a feature I wrote in *Autocar* magazine in 2003. Its conclusions were speculative at the time, but I managed to make the right call at the end of the day. The British Grand Prix survived.

So what's it all about, this spat over the British Grand Prix? Is it simply the fact that the public toilets at Silverstone have been a national disgrace for the past twenty years? Or the fact that some people who bought tickets to watch Alberto Ascari in 1953 are still queuing on the Dadford road to get into the track? No.

Is it that Bernie Ecclestone, motor racing's ultimate self-made man, is contemptuous of what he regards as the blue blazered toffs who run the British Racing Drivers' Club, the circuit's owners? Or genuinely that Bernie and the BRDC believes that government funding should be deployed to save the race? Not really.

In fact, it has precious little to do with any of the above. They are secondary considerations, tangential issues. The real problem for Silverstone is that its promoters, Brands Hatch Circuits (formerly Octagon Motorsports), are committed to a contract with Ecclestone's FOM organisation which hangs like an albatross around its neck.

In a nutshell, the promoters cannot

make money out of the British Grand Prix. And this is not because the BRDC will not agree to provide the funding to upgrade the circuit. That is another secondary issue. This problem has been caused because Ecclestone hiked the cost of the British GP quite dramatically when the last contract ended in 2001. And the people who signed up for it are buckling under its crippling cost. Bernie's companies will have earned more than £100m if the race survives to 2015, so he badly wants it to keep going.

The seeds of this conflict began in the spring of 1999 when Brands Hatch Leisure plc formulated an offer to run the British Grand Prix at Brands Hatch. The deal was cut between Ecclestone and Nicola Foulston, the feisty boss of Brands Hatch Leisure and the daughter of millionaire computer magnate John Foulston, who had been killed testing a McLaren Indy car at Silverstone in 1987.

Silverstone was balking at the cost of negotiating a new contract to hold the British Grand Prix from 2002 onwards. But Foulston, gambling that she could get planning permission to rebuild Brands Hatch to F1 standards, offered to sign up with Ecclestone.

Suddenly the cost of running the

British GP vaulted from £5m a year to over £8m a year with 10 per cent compound interest escalators which could see the race costing as much as £25m by the end of the current contract in twelve years' time.

Foulston also offered to buy Silverstone as a back-up contingency plan. It never happened and in January 2000 Foulston resigned as CEO of Brands Hatch — by which time the company had been sold to Octagon, a subsidiary of the US Interpublic group, for £120m. Foulston's personal share was about £25m.

Put simply — and despite whatever they may say to the contrary — Interpublic's subsidiary paid way over the odds for the company. As Jackie Stewart, the BRDC president, shrewdly observed at the time: 'You wouldn't see Warren Buffet doing things like this. They over-invested and didn't have the management team to handle it. Clearly, Octagon did inadequate due diligence when they started on this programme.

'That said, we have received assurances from the highest level within Interpublic that there is no question of them doing anything but honouring that contract.'

The bottom line is that Ecclestone and Mosley want the new pit complex to be built, as originally agreed, between Club and Abbey curve. This was put on hold when the main priority became successfully uprating the road access to Silverstone, about the only element in the plan which all the parties involved agree has been successfully carried out.

Now the money has to be found to press on with that rebuilding process. Mosley — ironically an honorary member of the BRDC — has carefully avoided explaining precisely how the FIA could remove a round of the F1 world championship from the international calendar when it has a perfectly valid commercial contract with FOM and a fully licenced race track on which to stage it.

The FIA president also suggested last week that the BRDC should not simply reduce its rent, but forgo it in its entirety for the next couple of years. 'If they receive £5m, that's an awful lot of money for a disused airfield which they got for free,' he said waspishly last week. Max is bit rusty on his history, incidentally, as the BRDC purchased the circuit progressively up to 1970.

So what happens in the end? It is all quite simple really.

At the end of the day a deal will be cut

to ensure the future of the British Grand Prix. Ecclestone will help mitigate Interpublic's losses by helping with finance for the new pit complex which, in turn, will help guarantee the race's position on the calendar by giving it the facilities it needs at a crucial moment.

The East Midlands Development Agency will be given the all clear to pitch in with a relatively small amount of indirect government support — and the BRDC will be prevailed upon to reduce its rent as a significant symbolic gesture to help massage the whole deal neatly together.

Yet it is important to remember that the main purpose of this exercise will be to help Brands Hatch Circuits in its battle to make sense of a contract which its parent company should have run a mile from at the outset.

At the end of the day, for all their professed lack of sentiment, neither Mosley nor Ecclestone will ditch the British Grand Prix as they won't want to be remembered as the people who scrapped one of the most historically significant events on the F1 calendar.

Neither of them would want to admit it. But that's the way it is.

PODIUM CEREMONIES
WHICH WENT WRONG

You'd have thought that it was all sufficiently straightforward. The top three finishers in a world championship Grand Prix appear on the rostrum standing on their appointed positions. They then receive their trophies from the appointed dignitaries. Everybody applauds, showers the champagne — unless you're in Bahrain, of course — and the drivers go home clutching their precious trophies. Couldn't be simpler. Or could it?

— 2006 TURKISH GP, ISTANBUL —

The long-term future of the Turkish Grand Prix at Istanbul was thrown into doubt only hours after the race was officially included on the FIA world championship calendar for 2007.

The sport was rocked by a major controversy after the Turkish Cypriot leader Mehmet ali Talat presented the winner's trophy at the 2006 event to the Ferrari driver Felipe Massa, deliberately flouting the protocol that the trophies are handed out by dignitaries from the host nation at the individual race.

To make matters worse, Talat was introduced as the president of the Turkish Cypriot state, which is recognised only by Turkey. Cyprus has been divided since 1974, when the Turkish military occupied the northern sector of the island after a Greek-supported coup.

The controversy was further fuelled by comments from Murat Yalcintas, the head of the Istanbul chamber of commerce. 'You cannot put a price on such promotion [of the Cyprus cause]', he told the Anatolia news agency. 'The Formula 1 race was a great opportunity. Cyprus is our national cause.'

— 1997 EUROPEAN GRAND PRIX, JEREZ —

After the row following the 1997 European Grand Prix, where the mayor of Jerez forced his way onto the podium uninvited, the F1 fraternity never again visited the circuit in southern Spain.

You could say this was the perfect end to a perfect day which had seen Jacques Villeneuve clinch the world championship for Williams, despite the efforts of Michael Schumacher to drive him off the road in his Ferrari. Schumacher lost all his world championship points as a result. But not the GP wins he scored. It was a meaningless penalty.

— 2002 Austrian Grand Prix, A1 Ring —

The Ferrari team was also fined $1m after an infringement of the podium procedure at the 2002 Austrian Grand Prix, where Rubens Barrichello took the top spot after relinquishing the victory to his team-mate Michael Schumacher coming out of the final corner.

It was a measure of how far out of touch the Ferrari team had become with the ordinary race fans that neither Schumacher nor Maranello team principal Jean Todt seemed to understand just how infuriated the jeering fans really were at this staged result.

— 1977 Japanese Grand Prix, Mount Fuji —

One year after clinching the world championship with a fourth place finish in the '76 race at Fuji, James Hunt returned to the Japanese circuit to win commandingly in his McLaren M26 ahead of Carlos Reutemann's Ferrari and Patrick Depailler's Tyrrell. At the end of the race, through sheer bloodymindedness dressed up as anxiety to catch a flight back to Europe, both Hunt and Reutemann refused to mount the podium, leaving Depailler to celebrate his third place alone.

No penalties were exacted and too many introspective FI insiders regarded the whole episode as a huge laugh. The hospitable Japanese were aghast at this lack of manners, but the FIA — an arthritic anachronism in those days — did nothing by way of imposing punishment. Small wonder that another ten years would pass before FI returned to Japan.

— 1982 SAN MARINO GRAND PRIX —

This was one podium ceremony which should have been a moment of unbridled joy, coming as it did at the end of an afternoon which had delivered a Ferrari 1-2, yet in reality it has come to be seen as a dreadful harbinger of doom for both the key players involved. Gilles Villeneuve had been leading the race ahead of his team-mate Didier Pironi at the moment when the two bright red cars assumed first and second position at the head of the field. It was established Maranello practice that the cars would hold those positions under such circumstances, but Pironi ratted on the deal, overtook Villeneuve and took the win. The look of shell-shocked dismay on the Canadian's face as he climbed the podium said it all. Two weeks later he was dead, killed practising for the Belgian GP at Zolder. Pironi would be invalided out of F1 later that year after crashing in practice for the German GP at Hockenheim, and was killed powerboating off the Isle of Wight five years afterwards.

How Team Orders Affected the Outcome of a World Championship

Team orders used to be an absolutely integral element in the battle for F1 honours. No question about it. But then the FIA decided to muddy the waters — yet again — in the mid-1990s, effectively decreeing that, er, well, it's OK for a team-mate to help another in the event of a world championship being at stake. But probably not otherwise. What they really meant, of course, was: 'We'll keep this as a tantalisingly imprecise grey area which will enable us to ensure that the rule means whatever we want it to mean in any particular circumstance.' All of which merely served to fray the competing teams' nerve ends as they grappled with such an unpredictable situation.

— 1958 FERRARI —

In the closing stages of the Moroccan Grand Prix at Casablanca, Ferrari signalled that Phil Hill, who was running second, should relinquish his position to Mike Hawthorn. Even though Stirling Moss won the race for Vanwall, Hawthorn clinched the title with 42 points to Moss's 41.

— 1964 FERRARI —

After Jim Clark's Lotus retired from the lead of the Mexican GP, Lorenzo Bandini dropped back from second place, allowing his team-mate John Surtees through into the runner-up spot behind Dan Gurney's winning Brabham. Surtees was thus champion, one point ahead of BRM team leader Graham Hill.

— 1978 LOTUS —

Mario Andretti and Ronnie Peterson were paired as team-mates in the all-conquering

Lotus 79s with the American ace cast in the deserved role of team leader while Ronnie duly rode shotgun in support. By the time Mario finished the title battle he was thirteen points ahead of the popular Swede, who tragically died from injuries sustained in the Italian GP at Monza.

— 1979 FERRARI —

Ferrari standing team orders were clear-cut at this stage in the team's history. Whoever was ahead at the point that the cars moved into first and second places would retain that position unchallenged. Following in the wheel tracks of his team-mate Jody Scheckter in the Italian GP, Gilles Villeneuve knew he only had to overtake him to clinch the title. But he was an honourable man, stayed second and lost the championship by four points to his colleague.

— 1997 McLaren and Williams —

In the closing stages of the 1997 European GP at Jerez, Jacques Villeneuve, who was driving for Williams, was instructed by his team to drop back to third behind the McLarens of

Mika Hakkinen and David Coulthard, paying back a favour earlier conferred by the McLaren team, who scheduled their refuelling stops to keep out of the Canadian's way as he battled Michael Schumacher's Ferrari for the title. Interestingly, in 2006 the Argentinian driver Norberto Fontana — who was driving a Ferrari-engined Sauber in that race — claimed that Ferrari boss Jean Todt came to the Sauber garage prior to the race, suggesting that the team drivers should block Villeneuve if they had the opportunity in order to favour Schumacher. Why Fontana waited so long to make that revelation remains a mystery.

— 2000—2004 Ferrari —

This era is simple. Michael Schumacher exercised his contractual *droit-de-seigneur* to dominate five straight world championships, with the supplicant Rubens Barrichello permitted to win only when it didn't interfere with Schuey's pressing priorities.

CONSECUTIVE DEBUT VICTORIES

When Jenson Button (Honda) and Felipe Massa (Ferrari) scored consecutive maiden career victories in the 2006 Hungarian and Turkish Grands Prix, all the amateur F1 statisticians in the media centre — author included — hailed this as a very rare event. Er, well, apart from the other twelve such consecutive pairings since the start of the world championship in 1950.

They were:

1950 British GP (Giuseppe Farina)
and
Monaco GP (Juan Manuel Fangio)

1951 British GP (Froilan Gonzalez)
and
German GP (Alberto Ascari)

1959 Monaco GP (Jack Brabham)
and
Dutch GP (Jo Bonnier)

1962 Belgian GP (Jim Clark)
and
French GP (Dan Gurney)

1968 French GP (Jacky Ickx)
and
British GP (Jo Siffert)

1973 French GP (Ronnie Peterson)
and
British GP (Peter Revson)

1974 South African GP (Carlos Reutemann)
and
Spanish GP (Niki Lauda)

1977 Belgian GP (Gunnar Nilsson)
and
Swedish GP (Jacques Laffite)

1980 South African GP (René Arnoux)
and
US West GP (Nelson Piquet)

1982 German GP (Patrick Tambay)
and
Austrian GP (Elio de Angelis)

1982 Austrian GP (Elio de Angelis)
and
Swiss GP (Keke Rosberg)

2003 Malaysian GP (Kimi Raikkonen)
and
Brazilian GP (Giancarlo Fisichella)

THE ONE THAT GOT AWAY

The McLaren-Honda squad won a record fifteen out of sixteen races in 1988, and would have achieved a clean sweep had not Ayrton Senna tripped over tough guy Jean-Louis Schlesser's Williams as he was lapping the slower car in the Italian GP. But if Ayrton expected an apology he was sadly mistaken ...

After the race, I was in the McLaren motorhome waiting to talk to Ron Dennis. Ayrton was there, sitting at one end like some furious potentate, and he had summoned Schlesser to appear before him. A relaxed Jean-Louis ambled in. 'What the bloody hell did you think you were doing?' barked the Brazilian. 'It was all your fault', replied Schless, almost amiably, before turning on his heels and walking out.

As for the actual incident, it was Ayrton's fault, as I was reminded by my old friend Eric Silbermann who was then the Honda PR man, as the Williams driver did all he could to get out of the way. In mitigation, though, Senna had been forced to push very hard by team-mate Prost until the Frenchman retired. So by the time he found himself leading, Senna was low on fuel and knew he had to maintain momentum if he was to finish and win, and he certainly couldn't afford to spend any time behind the much slower Judd-powered Williams — hence the hurried attempt to slide past at the chicane when he might have done better to wait for a straight.

Baby Boomers Invade F1

This is one of my favourite columns, which I wrote for the *Red Bulletin* at the 2006 Turkish Grand Prix on the occasion of BMW-Sauber new boy Sebastian Vettel becoming the youngest-ever participant in an F1 weekend.

'Youth is wasted on the young,' noted George Bernard Shaw sagely. He later added: 'Youth is such a wonderful thing, what a crime to waste it on children.' A somewhat less intellectual dimension was offered by a paddock insider who, on viewing the apparent arrival of a twelve-year-old in the pit lane climbing into a BMW-Sauber cockpit at the start of first practice here at Istanbul Park, added 'presumably when they reach puberty, they sack them.'

The cynic was referring to the arrival on the F1 scene of the fresh-faced Sebastian Vettel who, at 19 years 53 days, claimed the distinction of becoming the youngest ever driver to participate in a Grand Prix weekend in the 57-year history of the official World Championship. No, no, listen. Read my lips. I didn't say *competed* in a Grand Prix — and I know that Friday free practice for third drivers is a recently contrived F1 aberration — but the fact remains that the pleasant, if understandably rather shy, Vettel struck another blow for the sport's burgeoning youth culture. At this rate — and assuming he's any good — he could either be racing F1 for another 25 years or retired and sipping Martinis on the poop deck of his super yacht long before he celebrates his 30th birthday.

It really is a mad, mad world. Back in 1998 before his 21st birthday, McLaren had to send a driver to collect Nick Heidfeld from Heathrow when he was arriving for a Silverstone test. He was too young to sign for a hire car. Similarly, I'd like to monitor the blood pressure of any insurance broker on the end of a phone line dealing with a request from a 19-year-old attempting to arrange cover on a BMW M5.

'Well, Mr Vittal, how do you sell — sorry, I mean *spell* that? And your occupation? Grand Prix driver? Ah yes, of course ... [hand over mouthpiece] Hey Jack, it's that loopy kid again ...'

I must say that I'm right with David Coulthard on this whole issue of pushing youngsters along too fast and too soon. RBR's lead driver made the point that poor Christian Klien had been rushed into F1 too quickly 'and therefore hasn't had the chance to show his talent.' On the other hand you can understand the fear and trepidation in the minds of a youngster fearful of being branded 'over the top' at 24, a truly absurd state of affairs fuelled by too many karting kids testing an F3 car at Oscherslaben, or some other God-forsaken backwater, and immediately concluding they are the next Fernando Alonso. We are in danger of valuing precocious impetuosity above proven talent.

Of course, I have always prided myself on keeping a firm focus on all emergent young stars, monitoring their progress with a gimlet eye. This goes back to the mid-1980s when, at one German Grand Prix, I was leaving the Hockenheim TV boxes which were situated high in the back of the huge grandstand opposite the pits. Exiting amidst the crush of the paying public, I drew my colleague Nigel Roebuck's attention to the fact that some generous-minded father had fitted out his ten-year-old son in neatly tailored miniature Minardi team overalls.

Roebuck sighed with exasperation. 'I think you'll find that's Pierluigi Martini,' he said. I like to think he may have been joking. Except he wasn't.

WHY DO I NEVER LEARN?

You might be forgiven for wondering what I'm doing reporting in F1 on the basis of that contribution for the *Red Bulletin*. But how's this for confusion, as recounted in one of my regular 'Racing Line' columns published in *Autocar* in the summer of 2006?

Why is it I never learn? It's only two years since I engaged Gianmaria Bruni in conversation at the Bahrain GP in the bafflingly mistaken belief that I was talking to Zsolt Baumgartner, and last week I blundered into a similar *faux pas* while down in Stuttgart visiting the superb new Mercedes museum.

Got chatting to DTM Merc driver Susie Stoddart and casually inquired how she felt after flipping an F3 car at Rockingham a couple of years back. Her eyes narrowed quizzically as she politely corrected me. 'I think you need to talk to Katherine Legge about that, actually,' she said with the patient indulgence of a twenty-something addressing a half witted senior citizen.

Stoddart is enjoying her debut season driving a two-year-old C-class in Germany's prestige touring car series and was on parade doing promotional work at the German GP with her Mercedes team-mates Jamie Green, Bruno Spengler and Daniel la Rosa, all of whom had just come out of an action-packed Norisring DTM round the previous week-end.

Spengler won after Green, who started from pole, was pushed off the road by Audi driver Christian Abt while Stoddart got punted off after La Rosa tanked into the side of her with brake failure. I was impressed with just how much fun this quartet seemed to be deriving from their racing and how well they got on together.

La Rosa, an engaging young German, told me that the fans are always confusing him with Pedro de la Rosa, and even overall manufacturers Sparco recently rang him to say that his McLaren F1 driving suit was ready. Confusing racing drivers, can you imagine it? I think I'll keep quiet for now.

The Eight Youngest Drivers to Compete in a Grand Prix Weekend

---

Sebastian Vettel (D), born 3.7.87
Nineteen years, one month, 23 days (2006 Turkish GP)

Mike Thackwell (NZ), born 30.3.61
Nineteen years, five months, 29 days (1980 Canadian GP)

Ricardo Rodriguez (Mex), born 14.2.42
Nineteen years, six months, 27 days (1961 Italian GP)

Fernando Alonso (Esp), born 29.7.81
Nineteen years, seven months, four days (2001 Australian GP)

Esteban Tuero (Arg), born 22.4.78
Nineteen years, eleven months, fourteen days (1998 Australian GP)

Chris Amon (NZ), born 20.7.43
Nineteen years, eleven months, twenty days
(1963 Belgian GP)

Jenson Button (GB), born 1.9.80
Twenty years, one month, 22 days (2000
Australian GP)

Eddie Cheever (USA), born 10.1.56
Twenty years, one month, 23 days (1978 South
African GP)

HELMUT MARKO TESTS AN F1
McLAREN — OR DOES HE?

Today Helmut Marko is the Red Bull advisor
on young drivers, but in the early 1970s he was
regarded by many of his fellow Austrians as a
rising star in his own right, possibly with even
more potential than his compatriot Niki
Lauda who, as we all know, went on to win
three world championships.

Helmut, a lawyer from Graz, made it into
F1 as a member of the BRM team in 1972, only
for his career to end cruelly when a stone was

kicked up through his helmet visor during the French GP at Clermont-Ferrand, blinding him in one eye. No question about it, this was an F1 career cut short in its prime.

Marko was at the centre of one of the most amusing misunderstandings of my journalistic career. I flew back with him from an F2 race in Madrid during the summer of 1971. In those distant days before the advent of EasyJet and Ryanair it wasn't always possible to make direct flights across Europe from A to B. On this occasion we were both routed through Frankfurt, me to Heathrow and Helmut to Vienna.

Later that day I was back in the editorial office at *Motoring News* working on the news pages, when an excited reader rang in. 'Helmut Marko has been testing a McLaren M19 at Goodwood this very afternoon', he said breathlessly. 'I've got some photographs. Would you like them?'

Slightly unsettled, I replied: 'Are you sure?' He insisted that he was, adding: 'He's got his name on the side of his helmet!' I was intrigued, but the moment the photos arrived I instantly understood how he'd got his wires crossed. But he was almost right about the helmet, which carried the legend 'Mark' on both sides.

It was US racing ace Mark Donohue, testing in preparation for driving the car in the forthcoming Canadian GP!

The World Champions

I suppose no compendium of Grand Prix facts and figures would be complete without profiles of all the world champions since the inauguration of the official title chase in 1950. Yet the truth is we all know what they did. But what were they really like as individuals? These potted histories attempt to provide some answers.

1950 Giuseppe Farina (I)

b. 30.10.1906, Turin, Italy; d. 30.6.1966, nr Chambéry, France

33 Grands Prix, five wins

Career span: 1950–51 (Alfa Romeo); 1952–55 (Ferrari)

Aloof and distant, Farina was something of a

cold fish who had few friends at the top level of
motorsport. He never visited injured rivals in
hospital, and throughout his own career,
which was punctuated by accidents, he never
expected them to afford him the compliment
either. Back in the 1930s, collisions between
Farina and Marcel Lehoux (at Deauville) and
Lazlo Hartmann (at Tripoli) had resulted in
the deaths of both his rivals.

He raced the legendary Alfa 158s under
the Scuderia Ferrari banner before the war,
and it was at the wheel of one of these straight-
eight 1.5-litre supercharged monsters that he
clinched the first official world championship
in 1950 with wins in the British, Swiss and
Italian GPs. After this title success, Farina's
career dropped away steadily through to his
retirement at the end of the 1955 season
during which he competed in only a handful
of races, the lingering acute discomfort from
burns suffered at Monza the previous year only
partly allayed by pain-killing drugs.

Farina was driving a Lotus-Cortina on his way to the 1966 French GP when he crashed fatally into two telegraph poles after being caught out on a slippery road surface in the mountains near Chambéry just a few months short of his 60th birthday.

1951, 1954, 1955, 1956, 1957 JUAN MANUEL FANGIO (ARG)

b. 24.6.1911, Balcarce, Argentina; d. 17.7.1995, Balcarce

51 Grands Prix, 24 wins

Career span: 1950–51 (Alfa Romeo); 1953 (Maserati); 1954 (Maserati and Mercedes-Benz); 1955 (Mercedes-Benz); 1956 (Ferrari); 1958 (Maserati)

He was F1 racing's senior citizen, respected and revered as an icon from another era. Well into his eighties, his arrival in the pit lane was greeted with awe and reverential respect. Right to the end of his long life, Fangio was trim, dignified and radiated considerable presence.

This is not to say that Fangio was soft or over-sentimental. He was pragmatic; hard when he needed to be, but a sensitive and rather reserved gentleman away from the cockpit. He expected no favours and delivered few in return, but he had an overwhelming sense of sportsmanship and fair play. Although he was moved almost to tears by British driver Peter Collins's gesture in relinquishing his Lancia-Ferrari at Monza in 1956, by the same token there was no way he would ever offer a sliver of criticism in the direction of his other team-mate Luigi Musso for failing to relinquish his steed.

Yet at the end of the day it was the scale of Fangio's achievement which stood as the ultimate testimony to his unique genius. It's not the fact that Fangio won 24 Grands Prix which is so amazing — Jim Clark, Alain Prost, Niki Lauda, Ayrton Senna and Michael Schumacher all topped that total — but the fact that he did that in a career covering just 51 races.

That ensured that the serene man from the provincial Argentinian town won over 47 per cent of the Grands Prix he ever contested

— a statistic which will almost certainly remain unmatched in F1 history.

1952, 1953 ALBERTO ASCARI (I)

b. 13.7.1918, Turin; d. 26.5.1955, Monza

32 Grands Prix, thirteen wins

Career span: 1950–53 (Ferrari); 1954 (Maserati, Ferrari and Lancia); 1955 (Lancia)

One of Milan's favourite sons, Alberto Ascari was born into a motor racing family and is regarded as a greater driver than even the legendary Juan Manuel Fangio who was his great contemporary and rival in the early 1950s. He was killed during an impromptu test of a Ferrari sports car at Monza, by coincidence on the same day of the same month as his father Antonio died contesting the 1926 French GP at Montlhéry. Indeed, an idiosyncratic sub-culture subsequently developed in an attempt to attach a deeper significance to these two unrelated facts.

Ascari's domination of the 2-litre world championship in 1952 and 1953 was total. Armed with the superb little Ferrari 500 he won the '52 European GP at Spa, then pretty much swept all before him through to the end of the following year. He then signed to drive the forthcoming new Lancia D50 the following year, but spent most of the season sitting on the sidelines twiddling his thumbs while the car was finally completed.

The following year he was poised to take the lead of the Monaco GP when he crashed spectacularly at the waterfront chicane and ended up taking a ducking in the harbour. The following week he was killed at Monza. He was a quiet, pleasant and universally popular man as well as a formidable competitor. It was left for Fangio to bestow the ultimate accolade. 'I have lost my greatest opponent', he said quietly.

1958 MIKE HAWTHORN (GB)

b. 10.4.1929, Mexborough, Yorkshire; d. 22.1.1959, Guildford bypass

45 Grands Prix, three wins

Career span: 1952 (Cooper); 1953–54

(Ferrari); 1955 (Vanwall and Ferrari); 1956
(BRM, Maserati and Vanwall); 1957–58
(Ferrari)

Almost 50 years have passed since the death of
Britain's first F1 world champion in a road
accident only a few months after announcing
his retirement from driving, and there are
still a few of his contemporaries alive who
will testify to Mike's gregarious character and
talent behind the wheel.

Yet the more I hear about Hawthorn the
more I'm forced to conclude that he was
really a bit of a pain. OK, so he lived in
different times when boozing and carousing
were all part of the F1 driver's repertoire, but
if one flips through his memoirs *Challenge Me
the Race* and *Champion Year*, he comes across as a
tiresomely self-indulgent character wedded to
his own small coterie of close friends.

Truth be told, he was a pretty inconsistent
F1 driver, good on his day but not in the same

class as Vanwall team-mates Stirling Moss and Tony Brooks, both of whom he beat to the title crown. That said, Hawthorn certainly caught the public's imagination with his wheel-to-wheel between his Ferrari and Juan Manuel Fangio's Maserati for victory in the 1953 French GP at Reims.

Hawthorn was also unfortunate in being hounded by the sensational end of the British daily newspaper market, being accused of dodging his national service, and this matter concerning one of England's most high-profile sportsmen even prompted discussions in the House of Commons. In truth, Mike suffered from a kidney ailment which would almost certainly have rendered him ineligible, but the fact remained that a broad swathe of public opinion could not reconcile this reality with the fact that he was fit enough to race F1 cars.

1959, 1960, 1966 JACK BRABHAM (AUS)

b. 2.4.1926, Hurstville, nr Sydney, Australia

126 Grands Prix, fourteen wins

Career span: 1955–61 (Cooper); 1962–70 (Brabham)

1966

Down-to-earth, undemonstrative and over-whelmingly practical. That pretty well sums up the key qualities deployed by Jack Brabham throughout a career which not only yielded him three world championship crowns, but also the distinction of winning his third title in 1966 at the wheel of a car bearing his own name.

This was a feat destined to stand unequalled in F1 history, but it was typical of Brabham that he modestly played down the magnitude of his achievement, gaining considerable satisfaction from the fact that many observers reckoned he was over the hill at 40 when he clinched that third championship. In fact Brabham raced on to the end of the 1970 season, when he finally hung up his helmet at the age of 44 and concentrated on his other business interests.

Jack Brabham is recalled by all who worked with him as a man who never wasted his words; monosyllabic replies were the most even his closest friends could expect in the F1 pit lane. But he was shrewd to the point of sheer cunning, a great mechanical improviser and an all-rounder prepared to turn his hand to any chore if the necessity arose.

Even his team-mates Dan Gurney and Denny Hulme recalled that Jack played his cards really close to his chest and that they never quite knew what technical tweaks he had up his sleeve to turn to his own advantage.

1961 PHIL HILL (USA)

b. 20.4.1927, Miami, Florida

48 Grands Prix, three wins

Career span: 1958–62 (Ferrari); 1963 (ATS); 1964 (Cooper); 1965 (Centro Sud)

Many people shared the view that this pleasant Californian was simply too intelligent to be a racing driver, let alone to work for Enzo Ferrari at a time when the Italian team boss was at the absolute peak of his cantankerous powers. Although born in Florida, Phil was brought up in Santa Monica, a genteel, leafy enclave of Los Angeles suburbia fronting onto the Pacific Ocean.

One of only two Americans to take the crown, he secured the 1961 title with victory in Ferrari's home race which was tragically marred by the death of his team-mate Wolfgang von Trips and fourteen spectators when the German count's car flew into the crowd after colliding with Jim Clark's Lotus.

Hill's F1 career continued in a gentle decline until the end of 1965, but he continued racing sports cars for another two years, rounding off his 1967 season with a fine victory in the BOAC 1,000-km endurance event, sharing the distinctive winged Chaparral with Britain's Mike Spence.

At the start of the following year, the quiet and introspective gentleman suddenly remembered that he had forgotten to renew his international competition licence and, in his own words, 'found that I had become a retired racing driver'.

1962, 1968 GRAHAM HILL (GB)

b. 15.2.1929, Hampstead, London; d. 29.11.1975, Arkley, nr London

176 Grands Prix, fourteen wins

Career span: 1958–59 (Lotus); 1960–66 (BRM); 1967–70 (Lotus); 1971–72 (Brabham); 1973–75 (Embassy Hill)

My most vivid memories of Graham Hill centre around two trips I took with him in his Piper Aztec, the aeroplane in which he and five others — including rising star Tony Brise — would eventually die when it crashed in fog on Arkley golf course one winter night in 1975. Cruising across Europe en route to an F2 race at Salzburgring with the plane on auto-pilot and Graham dozing quietly behind his sunglasses certainly seemed a laid-back way to behave to a novice like me. His death eventually came as a result of acute over-confidence — call it arrogance, if you like — and these were qualities which defined the man behind the public persona to a considerable extent.

The well-trimmed moustache and the saucy wink had helped Hill become one of the country's most identifiable sporting stars throughout the 'Swinging Sixties' at a time when his on-track reputation was at its zenith. Yet behind Graham's beaming public demeanour lurked a less charitable side to his character. Away from his adoring fans he could be crushingly rude and also singularly irresponsible — it emerged after his death that the plane was not properly insured or registered. The bereaved families ended up having no option but to sue his estate for compensation.

1963, 1965 JIM CLARK (GB)

b. 4.3.1936, Kilmany, Fife, Scotland; d. 7.4.1968, Hockenheim

72 Grands Prix, 25 wins

Career span: 1960–68 (Lotus)

When Jim Clark died in a minor league F2 race at Hockenheim in the spring of 1968, the whole fabric of international motor racing trembled. Clark, more than anybody else in the history of the sport, had seemed totally inviolate.

Clark was a rather shy, self-effacing son of a Scottish border farmer who went motor racing primarily for his own pleasure. In so many ways he was the last great sporting 'amateur' driver, and he died just before the onset of unbridled commercialism — which he abhorred — in the sport he loved so passionately.

The record books show that he won the world championship in 1963 and 1965, but he came within a whisker of taking it in '62 and '64 as well. The fact of the matter is that he dominated all four seasons in a manner seldom matched since. The green Lotus with its yellow stripe and blue-helmeted driver won a total of 25 Grands Prix between 1962 and his death six years later, yet it was the manner of Clark's success which really demoralised his opposition.

Inevitably starting from pole position, he would destroy his competitors' spirit with a

Jim Clark

searing first lap which none of them could approach, let alone equal. He was the yardstick by which his contemporaries judged their own performance, and he had most of them psychologically beaten before they even climbed into their cars.

1964 JOHN SURTEES (GB)

b. 11.2.1934, Tatsfield, Surrey

III Grands Prix, six wins

Career span: 1960 (Lotus); 1961 (Cooper); 1963–66 (Ferrari); 1966 (Cooper); 1967–68 (Honda); 1969 (BRM); 1970–72 (Surtees)

John was a deeply committed and very serious-minded competitor. He won seven world championships on two wheels for the legendary MV Agusta motorcycle team before switching to cars in 1960 with brilliant effect. His empathy with all things Italian led to him joining Ferrari in 1963 and he sealed a world championship the following year, becoming the only man so far to win title crowns in both disciplines.

Surtees could be inspirational and frustrating to work for in equal measure. In that sense he was much like Nigel Mansell: imbued with huge self-belief and confident that his way of doing things was the only right way. In 1966 he would leave Ferrari after a falling-out with the Commendatore in circumstances which have never been satisfactorily explained. All that was certain is that this parting of the ways was a loss to both men.

John would score one more GP victory driving for Honda, but that was the sum total of his achievement. He built some good F1 and F2 cars in the early 1970s, but never scaled the upper peaks again. In many ways his was a career which was squandered. Sad to relate.

1967 DENNY HULME (NZ)

b. 18.6.1936, Nelson, South Island, NZ;
d. 4.10.1992, Mount Panorama, Australia

112 Grands Prix, eight wins

Career span: 1965–67 (Brabham); 1967–74 (McLaren)

Denny was a tough character from rural New

Zealand whose father Clive won a Victoria
Cross for his bravery at Anzio during the
Second World War. Denny clearly inherited
his father's resilience. Legend has it that during his youth he was doing some welding in his
father's garage when he smelled burning. It
appeared that he'd smelled it before he felt a
burning sensation in his foot. Later, in 1970,
he would bear the searing pain of methanol
burns – sustained while testing at Indianapolis
when a fuel filler worked loose on a McLaren
Indy car – without a murmur of complaint.

Denny came out of his patron Jack
Brabham's shadow to win the 1967 world
championships, taking just two race victories
at Monaco and Nürburgring along the way. He
very much learned his trade with the Brabham
squad, but in 1968 decided to switch to his
compatriot Bruce McLaren's emergent F2
operation. He would stay with McLaren until
the end of his career, helping to pull the team
back together again after the body blow of

Bruce's death while testing a Can-Am car at Goodwood in June 1970.

At the end of 1974 the manner of his retirement from driving was so low-key that it was only when he didn't appear for the first race of the following season that the F1 community was convinced he had finally gone. You crossed Denny Hulme at your peril, but if you managed to penetrate that granite edifice there was a warm-hearted character within. That he should ultimately die from a heart attack while racing a touring car seemed the ultimate irony.

1969, 1971, 1973 JACKIE STEWART (GB)

b. 11.6.1939, Dumbarton, Scotland

99 Grands Prix, 27 wins

Career span: 1965–67 (BRM); 1968–69 (Tyrrell Matra); 1970 (Tyrrell March and Tyrrell); 1971–73 (Tyrrell)

Thirty-four years have now passed since Jackie retired at the end of a career which yielded three world championships, but he is now more prominent a figure on the international motor racing scene than he ever was in his motor racing heyday. As one of the sport's most informed observers and influential advisors he has worked for a wide range of global corporations as an international sporting ambassador.

Yet such were Stewart's achievements in other areas of motorsport that it's all too easy to overlook his impressive racing career. Far more significant is the fact that he debunked the myth that racing drivers should be devil-may-care extroverts to whom death or injury was something they should embrace without question as an automatic part of their calling. He was the driving force behind sweeping safety improvements, an attitude which did not always find favour with the purists by whom he was much maligned as a result. He always made a very good friend and a very bad enemy.

More than two decades after his retirement from driving, a Stewart-Ford F1 car driven by Johnny Herbert won the 1999

European GP at Nürburgring. By Jackie's own admission it was a satisfying moment which came close to matching the emotion of his own visits to the F1 podium. And – as if to underline the fact that timing is everything in life – he sold the team to Ford at the end of that season.

1970 JOCHEN RINDT (Au)

b. 18.4.1942, Mainz-am-Rhein, Germany;
d. 5.9.1970, Monza

60 Grands Prix, six wins

Career span: 1964 (Rob Walker); 1965–67 (Cooper); 1968 (Brabham); 1969–70 (Lotus)

Rindt's parents were killed in a bombing raid on Hamburg when he was only a few weeks old, so he was brought up by his maternal grandparents in the Austrian city of Graz. He grew up with a wild and rebellious streak which ensured that he was an intensely independent operator for much of his career, brimming with self-confidence and natural talent.

Jochen exploded to the forefront of public attention by winning the 1964 London Trophy on the tight little Crystal Palace circuit, a summer afternoon on which he beat all the established stars and put his name in the frame as a likely tip for future success. Yet not until he drove for Lotus in 1969 did Jochen finally score his first GP victory after years of trying. He died at Monza practising for the following year's Italian GP when a brake shaft broke on his Lotus 72, leaving his wife Nina — a former international model — and a three-year-old daughter, Natascha. By then he had amassed sufficient points to ensure that he would claim the dubious distinction of becoming the sport's first — and so far thankfully only — posthumous world champion.

Jochen was also a close friend of Bernie Ecclestone, who negotiated his contracts with both the Brabham and Lotus teams. During his time at Lotus, Jochen and Bernie used to drive Colin Chapman round the bend by their habit of playing gin rummy right up to — and sometimes beyond — the moment when the

Lotus boss required his star driver to climb in the cockpit and strut his stuff. Most people who knew him felt that Jochen was a far-sighted businessman who could visualise a life well beyond F1. Probably in partnership with Bernie. Oh yes, and today Natascha Rindt flies the FIA's private Lear jet used by the governing body's president Max Mosley.

1972, 1974 EMERSON FITTIPALDI (BR)

b. 12.12.1946, São Paolo, Brazil

144 Grands Prix, fourteen wins

Career span: 1970–73 (Lotus); 1974-75 (McLaren); 1976–80 (Fittipaldi)

Emerson's father Wilson Fittipaldi senior was one of Brazil's foremost motor sporting journalists and broadcasters, stretching back to Fangio's emergent years racing in Europe in the early 1950s. That gave Emerson Fittipaldi the best possible launch pad for his own motor racing aspirations.

Wilson Snr and his wife Juzy encouraged the racing interests of both their sons, Emerson contesting no fewer than 144 Grand Prix starts and winning fourteen races on his way to two world championships, in 1972 (Lotus) and 1974 (McLaren). Later he was twice winner of the Indy 500. To this day, Emerson continues to exude huge charisma and star quality.

His grandson Pietro, son of his daughter Juliane, is now ten and racing karts while another daughter, Tatiana, is married to the one-time Arrows F1 driver Max Papis, and their son Mario Fittipaldi Papis was born in July 2006. Emerson's brother Wilson — three years his senior — contested 36 Grands Prix in the 1970s, his best placing being a fifth at Nürburgring just ahead of his brother in the 1973 German GP driving a Brabham BT42. Wilson junior's son Christian contested 40 Grands Prix, driving for both Minardi and Arrows with three fourth places to his credit, before moving to the USA where he has raced Champcars and NASCAR. Quite some dynasty for the delightful Emerson to rule over!

1975, 1977, 1984 Niki Lauda [Au]

b. 22.2.1949, Vienna

171 Grands Prix, 25 wins

Career span: 1971–72 (March); 1973 (BRM); 1974–77 (Ferrari); 1978–79 (Brabham); 1982–85 (McLaren)

Outwardly ascetic and rather formal, the true personality of Niki Lauda couldn't be further from this stereotyped image. Niki served his motor racing apprenticeship in the early 1970s when the offbeat humour of John Cleese and *Monty Python's Flying Circus* was very much in vogue. You might find it difficult to imagine a future triple world champion joining in with the March mechanics shouting 'albatross' or 'gannet on a stick', but you can take it from me that's how it was.

Niki shrugged aside his burns sustained at Nürburgring in 1976 with total stoicism. But he was deeply shaken by the crash of one of his

Lauda Air Boeing 767s over Thailand in 1992 with the loss of over 200 lives. 'If I want to risk my life in a racing car, that's one thing', he said. 'But if passengers buy a ticket on my airline and don't come back it's totally unacceptable.' The aircraft had suffered a failure, and he pursued Boeing on the matter of a legal settlement for all the victims with all the single-minded tenacity that he'd applied to his race driving.

1976 JAMES HUNT (GB)

b. 29.8.1947, Belmont, Surrey; d. 15.6.1993, Wimbledon

92 Grands Prix, ten wins

Career span: 1973–75 (Hesketh); 1976–78 (McLaren); 1979 (Wolf)

Niki Lauda can do this contribution.

'Ronnie Peterson was my team-mate at the time [1971] and he sort-of knew James who at that time was doing a lot of crashing in one of the March Formula 3 cars. But it was the connection with March that really enabled me to get to know James. He lived in Fulham, as I recall, and despite the fact we were pretty directly opposed competitors, we knocked around a lot together socially and became good friends.

'The truth of it was that I think we were both rebels to some extent. Our friendship was definitely strengthened by the fact that both our families were pretty seriously opposed to our being involved in motor racing. James's parents had told him pretty directly that they weren't prepared to fund his motor racing. But at least he didn't have a grandfather telephoning his potential sponsors telling them not to get involved with him, which was something that happened to me early on in my racing career.

'It was also fairly clear that, while I tended to be portrayed as the serious one among the group, beneath all that "Hunt the Shunt" image — which was nonsense, in my view — I quickly formed the view that James would be one of the guys I'd have to beat if and when we ever made our way up into F1.'

Only after his untimely and premature

death in 1993 did his friends come to appreciate the depths of depression and drug dependency against which James had battled in his latter years.

1978 MARIO ANDRETTI (USA)

b. 28.2.1940, Montana, Italy

128 Grands Prix, twelve wins

Career span: 1968–69 (Lotus); 1970 (March); 1971–72 (Ferrari); 1974–76 (Parnelli); 1976–80 (Lotus); 1981 (Alfa Romeo); 1982 (Williams and Ferrari)

Mario Andretti's life story has about it the essence of the great American dream. He was born near Trieste in the early months of the Second World War and his family spent the first seven years of his life in a displaced persons' camp, eventually emigrating to the USA in 1955.

Mario, brought up on a diet of Alberto

Ascari and the legendary Mille Miglia road race, later admitted that the prospect of leaving Italy horrified him. He thought he might never see motor racing again, but, as history happily relates, he and his brother Aldo picked up the threads of their passion for the sport once they arrived on the opposite side of the Atlantic.

Mario won the Indy 500 for his first and only time in 1969, triumphed in the '71 South African GP for Ferrari and went on to win the world championship for Lotus in 1978. One of the most versatile drivers ever to sit in a racing car, as well as one of the most civil and courteous, he was nevertheless no soft touch.

He had no compunction about overtaking his son Michael's misfiring machine on the run up to the chequered flag in the 1986 Portland CART race, prompting the younger Andretti to air the view that it might have been nice if his Old Man had allowed him to squeeze home the winner.

Mario's eyes narrowed. 'That's not the way it works, Michael', he said drily.

1979 Jody Scheckter (SA)

b. 29.1.1950, East London, South Africa

112 Grands Prix, ten wins

Career span: 1972–73 (McLaren); 1974–76 (Tyrrell); 1977–78 (Wolf); 1979–80 (Ferrari)

When he arrived in F1 as the McLaren team's raw and untutored rising star in 1972, Jody was quickly nicknamed 'Fletcher' after the baby seagull in the contemporary children's book *Jonathan Livingstone Seagull* who tried to fly at too early an age and kept crashing into the cliff face as a result.

From the outset 'Fletch' was undeniably world championship material, but he kept trying so hard that you really began to wonder whether or not the boy would survive long enough to make it. Single-handedly at Silverstone in 1973 he wiped out more than half the British GP field at the end of the opening lap. But he pulled everything together and really started to make his name as a serious contender with the Tyrrell squad the following year as Jackie Stewart's successor.

He spent three years with Tyrrell, then two driving for Walter Wolf's independent team. Finally at the start of 1979 he signed the two-year deal with Ferrari which would carry him to the world championship. Throughout that memorable '79 season he was partnered by the legendary Gilles Villeneuve, a driver with a very different personality than the South African, but a man with whom Jody bonded like a soulmate.

There was only one snag which caused tension between the two men. They both lived in Monaco and, when the call came for them to go to a Ferrari test at Fiorano, Scheckter's instinctive reaction was: 'I'll drive.' The only thing scarier than driving with Gilles was flying there in his helicopter. And Jody didn't want to do that either.

1980 Alan Jones (Aus)

b. 2.11.1946, Melbourne

116 Grands Prix, twelve wins

Career span: 1975 (Hesketh and Hill); 1976 (Surtees); 1977 (Shadow); 1978–81 (Williams); 1983 (Arrows); 1985–86 (Lola)

Alan Jones was admittedly an unlikely champion. His great days with Williams were somehow book-ended and shaded by Mario Andretti's high-profile championship for Lotus in '78 and the emergence of Alain Prost in the early 1980s. But let's be clear what we mean. It wasn't his talent and guts at the wheel over which there was any question. Once he established a foothold in the F1 business he unquestionably delivered. Yet in the junior formulae during the 1970s his star had never quite shone as brightly as those of Roger Williamson, Tom Pryce or Tony Brise. Ironically, he would outlive all three and get his big chance as a result of Pryce's tragic death in the 1977 South African GP at Kyalami.

Jones made that once-in-a-lifetime opportunity work for him. Wringing everything he could from the heavy Shadow DN8, Alan was in the right place at the right time when James Hunt's McLaren M26 suffered an engine failure at the Osterreichring. Victory in the Austrian GP fell into Alan's lap. He was on his way.

One of the men who was watching was Frank Williams. Frank was busy re-establishing himself in the FI business after selling the remnants of his original company to the Austro-Canadian oil magnate Walter Wolf. Now he was looking for a driver.

'Hans Stuck, Gunnar Nilsson and Alan were on our list', recalled Frank. 'All I can say is that if you work backwards over the years, you can see we've made all sorts of bum driver selections, but Jones was a great one.'

1981, 1983, 1987 NELSON PIQUET (BR)

b. 17.8.1952, Rio de Janeiro

204 Grands Prix, 23 wins

Career span: 1978 (Ensign and McLaren); 1979–85 (Brabham); 1986–87 (Williams); 1988–89 (Lotus); 1991–92 (Benetton)

This gifted Brazilian was born Nelson Sauto-

Maoir, but switched to using his mother's maiden name, Piquet, at an early stage in his career when he wanted to keep the fact that he was motor racing from his parents' attention. If his father had got his way, the young Nelson would have been coached for a life of professional tennis, but the youngster found the lure of high octane competition just too much to resist.

After making his way up from a grounding in kart racing, Nelson was dominating the British F3 championship scene by the end of 1978 and made some intermittent F1 outings with a couple of minor teams by the end of that year. Bernie Ecclestone quickly homed in on Nelson's innate talent, signing him to drive for the Brabham team from the start of 1979. He stayed there until the start of 1986 when — having won two world championships — he switched to the Williams-Honda squad alongside Nigel Mansell. Despite a tense and bitter rivalry with the feisty British driver, Nelson bagged another title before switching to Lotus, and later Benetton, where he finished his distinguished F1 career.

The Piquet/Mansell rivalry, intense though it was, always managed to contain itself one step short of physical confrontation. 'It once got out of hand in the cabin [team office] at Mexico City after the 1987 race when they slagged each other off face to face', said Frank Williams.

'They never came near to punch-ups, it was all "if you think that was close, wait until next time", but they were still pumped up after the race, the adrenalin was still flowing. They were professionals and realised they both had to cross the finishing line in order to score points.'

1982 KEKE ROSBERG (FIN)

b. 6.12.1948, Stockholm, Sweden

114 Grands Prix, five wins

Career span: 1978 (Theodore); 1979 (Wolf); 1980–81 (Fittipaldi); 1982–85 (Williams); 1986 (McLaren)

This son of a Finnish vet and amateur rally driver had come to front-line international racing quite late in the day. Lars Rosberg would have preferred his son to pursue a career in dentistry or computer programming, but was nevertheless supportive when Keke started kart racing in his teens.

In 1978, Keke won the rain-soaked Silverstone International Trophy race in the Theodore TR1 which was owned by Hong Kong-based entrepreneur Teddy Yip, a hugely enthusiastic and passionate motor racing enthusiast. Yet it would take more than another year before he seriously got his foot on the F1 ladder. After the 1979 Monaco Grand Prix, James Hunt decided to quit Walter Wolf's F1 team. And Keke got the job.

Wolf amalgamated with Fittipaldi and eventually closed its doors. But then a lifeline thrown by Frank Williams came in the form of an invitation to a test session at the Paul Ricard circuit in southern France late in 1981.

Williams was also testing the Frenchman Jean-Pierre Jarier as a possible candidate for the job as Carlos Reutemann's team-mate in 1982. But it was Keke who really excited talent scout Charlie Crichton-Stuart and the team's aerodynamicist Frank Dernie.

'It was obvious he was tremendously quick and determined from the outset', Charlie subsequently recounted. 'On our first night in the hotel down at Ricard he was up until one o'clock drinking with us, and the next morning Frank Dernie suggested: "Let's put this guy on qualifiers and tell him to go for it, without even a lap to warm up." So Keke appeared, bleary-eyed, drinking endless black coffees and smoking about half a dozen Marlboros at once. Into the car and snap! He was instantly quick. A blind, one-eyed monkey could have seen his potential.'

1985, 1986, 1989, 1993 ALAIN PROST (F)

b. 24.2.1955, Lorette, Saint-Chamond, nr St-Etienne

119 Grands Prix, 51 wins

Career span: 1980 (McLaren); 1981–83 (Renault); 1984–89 (McLaren); 1990–91 (Ferrari); 1993 (Williams)

1989

From an early stage in his career Alain Prost admitted that he modelled his smooth driving style on that of Jim Clark, so it was no surprise when his star shone brightly immediately from the moment he joined the Renault F1 team at the start of the 1981 season. In 1983 he was pipped for the drivers' title in the final race of the season by Piquet's Brabham-BMW despite having led for much of the season.

Extraordinarily, Prost was made the fall guy for the team's failure and was dropped from the squad at the end of the year. Many judged this to be an insane decision, permitting the McLaren boss Ron Dennis to jump in and sign Prost — at a bargain basement fee — to run alongside Niki Lauda the following year. But despite winning seven races to Niki's five, the Frenchman lost out by just half a point in the title battle. In 1985, though, he won the championship commandingly and repeated that achievement the following year, thereby becoming the first back-to-back champion since Jack Brabham in 1959–60.

Prost remained at McLaren until the end of 1989, the season in which he took his third title crown. Feeling that his position had been usurped by the arrival of the dynamically motivated Ayrton Senna at the start of 1988, he switched to Ferrari for 1990, where he had a similarly tempestuous partnership with Nigel Mansell. In 1992 he took a year's sabbatical, after which he returned to win a fourth world title in 1993 with Williams before retiring for good at the end of that year. By any standards his was a rare talent.

1988, 1990, 1991 Ayrton Senna (Br)

b. 21.3.1960, São Paolo; d. 1.5.1994, Bologna, Italy

161 Grands Prix, 41 wins

Career span: 1984 (Toleman); 1985–87 (Lotus); 1988–93 (McLaren); 1994 (Williams)

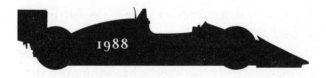

A lot of people concluded that Ayrton Senna was cold and aloof. But in fact he had an impish sense of humour which developed progressively throughout his time at McLaren from 1988 to 1992. Humour can be a great tension-breaker, and both Senna and team boss Ron Dennis certainly came to realise and appreciate the value of that as they faced up to the inevitable frustrations which are part and parcel of the F1 racing business.

So what made Ayrton so special as a driver? Well, apart from the obvious natural talent, he was physically fit to a level which caught many of his rivals off-guard. He would take one month a year off for relaxation and enjoying life in his native Brazil. Dedication and focus are today commonplace qualities in Formula 1, but during Ayrton's early years at McLaren his opposition suddenly realised that he had moved the goal posts as far as levels of commitment were concerned. He quickly became the person who set the standards for others to follow.

On a more personal level, much of his motivation had its roots in his devotion to his Brazilian background. Brazil has a unique culture which is based on a burning optimism about its future, even though it perhaps never quite realises the aspirations which it seeks. Yet no matter where he was in the world, Brazil was the magnet which drew him home time and again. His commitment to his family was also central to his life and that in itself reflected the very essence of the Brazilian ethos.

1992 Nigel Mansell (GB)

b. 8.8.1953, Upton-on-Severn, UK

187 Grands Prix, 31 wins

Career span: 1980–84 (Lotus); 1986–88
(Williams); 1989–90 (Ferrari); 1991–92
(Williams); 1994 (Williams); 1995 (McLaren)

Nigel Mansell was certainly a tough customer. A teenage karting star, he'd never quite mustered sufficient backing to break into the big time as he battled up through the junior formulae. His big break came in 1980 when Colin Chapman, the charismatic Lotus boss, offered him a chance of a test drive at the Paul Ricard circuit. He made his F1 debut in the Austrian GP that year, sitting in a bath of petrol for much of the race distance after his Lotus 81's fuel tank sprang a leak. He suffered in silence and the reward for his resilience came the following year when he was recruited to drive full-time for the team alongside the Italian Elio de Angelis.

The qualities in Mansell which persuaded Williams to give him a chance in 1985 were forged during those four problematical years with Lotus. Chapman had seen past Nigel's chippy and argumentative exterior and identified that this bullishly confident young man had a genuine talent. He also had the speed necessary to get the job done, but by the time his tenure with Lotus had come to an end, one was bound to wonder whether he had sufficient good luck to be a worthwhile bet.

Mansell spent three years with Williams, then switched to Ferrari for two years, decided to retire, changed his mind, returned to Frank's team to win the '92 title, fell out with him and left again, went to race CART, returned to F1 with Williams in 1994, then switched to McLaren in '95 only to leave the team after a handful of races. Exhausted after all that? Me too!

1994, 1995, 2001–04
MICHAEL SCHUMACHER (D)

b. 31.1.1969, Hurth-Hermulheim, Germany

249 Grands Prix, 91 wins

Career span; 1991 (Jordan and Benetton); 1992–95 (Benetton); 1996–2006 (Ferrari)

1994

Michael Schumacher's confidence was for years firmly buttressed by the unwavering support and confidence he enjoyed from a small group of hard-line Ferrari loyalists who believed that his unique talent enabled him to ride out the short-term disruptions generated by the ebb and flow of racing fortunes.

Michael's was an extraordinary talent, and the statistical record he wrote into the F1 history books is unlikely ever to be bettered. Yet despite being a devoted family man away from the circuit, once strapped into the cockpit of his car he was a ruthless and uncompromisingly competitive operator who took few hostages and was seldom far from the epicentre of any controversy which might be enveloping the sport at any particular time.

There are those who believe that he stayed around perhaps a couple of years too long. If Schumacher's reputation was blotted by his memorable collision with Damon Hill at Adelaide in 1994, or his tangle with Jacques Villeneuve at Jerez three years later, then the general consensus was that he had gone too far — even by his own standards — when he deliberately skidded to a halt in the middle of the track during qualifying at Monaco in 2006, thereby thwarting his rival Fernando Alonso's bid for pole position.

Yet Schumacher certainly deserves his place in the pantheon of motorsporting greats for the manner in which he helped revive the Ferrari team fortunes in the late 1990s, laying the foundations for the longest period of sustained success ever achieved by the Prancing Horse.

1996 Damon Hill (GB)

b. 17.9.1960, Hampstead, London

115 Grands Prix, 22 wins

Career span: 1993–96 (Williams); 1997 (Arrows); 1998–99 (Jordan)

Damon Hill's most impressive race came in

the pouring rain at Suzuka in 1994 when he out-foxed Michael Schumacher on a near-flooded circuit to win the Japanese Grand Prix in truly superb style. It was yet another example of how the serious-minded Londoner could raise the level of his game when the pressure was really on.

Hill's advancement through the F1 ranks was certainly fortunate, but he superbly capitalised on any opportunity which came his way. A test driving role with the Williams squad led to promotion to a race seat along-side Alain Prost in 1993 after Nigel Mansell decided he would pursue a career on the US Champcar scene. In 1994 he picked up the baton for Williams after Ayrton Senna's death, losing his chance of the title after Schumacher helped him off the road in Adelaide, but two years later finally took the championship.

Although he subsequently raced for Arrows and Jordan, it will be for his four years at Williams that Damon will best be remembered. He was not to be stopped in 1996. He started the year with three straight wins at Melbourne, Interlagos and Buenos Aires, after which his Williams FW18 stormed to further victories at Imola, Montreal, Magny-Cours, Hockenheim and in the season finale at Suzuka. In the process Damon had fought off a mounting challenge from Villeneuve which went all the way to the final race.

So what was his reward? A lucrative new contract for 1997? A generous multi-million-dollar success bonus? No, none of those things. Damon's reward for those efforts was to be dropped from the team by Frank Williams.

F1 can certainly sometimes be a funny old world.

1997 Jacques Villeneuve (Can)

b. 9.4.1971, Saint Jean Richelieu, Chambly, Quebec

162 Grands Prix, eleven wins

Career span: 1996–98 (Williams); 1999–2003 (BAR); 2004 (Renault); 2005–06 (Sauber and BMW-Sauber)

After many later successes in America — becoming CART champion, winning the Indianapolis 500 — Villeneuve came to FI in 1996, with Williams-Renault. At Melbourne he became only the third driver to start his first Grand Prix from pole position, and only an engine problem kept him from winning the race.

At the end of that year, Patrick Head — the Williams technical director — considered the team's latest star. 'As a driver, he reminds me a little bit of Piquet, in that he's very, very in control in the cockpit, as Nelson was. You'd be thinking, "Why isn't he going faster?" In fact, he was just doing his homework, working away — but then when it was time go faster, he could just dive into it. I don't think Jacques gets flustered very easily.

'As a bloke, I think he's a bit of a one-off, really. Very self-contained. Maybe he needs Jock Clear, his race engineer, in his camp, but the impression he gives is that he doesn't really need the rest of us. It's almost as if he doesn't want to make any form of bond with the team — or with people generally, although he's got certain "insiders". You'd have to say he's very self-confident.'

Second to team-mate Damon Hill in the '96 world championship, Villeneuve went one better the following year, and in circumstances to make you believe maybe there is a God, after all. In the title-deciding race at Jerez, Michael Schumacher led, but Jacques reeled him in; when he went for the lead, Schumacher tried to take him out. For once, happily, the biter was bitten back.

1998, 1999 MIKA HAKKINEN (FIN)

b. 28.9.1968, Helsinki

161 Grands Prix, twenty wins

Career span: 1991–92 (Lotus); 1993–2001 (McLaren)

You just knew that Mika was made of the right stuff when he outqualified his McLaren team leader Ayrton Senna for the 1993 Portuguese GP at Estoril. Concealing his irritation, Ayrton had to admit that he was impressed.

Seven years later the Finn pulled the overtaking move of the decade at Spa-Francorchamps as he and Michael Schumacher went either side of Ricardo Zonta's BAR-Honda as they lapped the slower car. Concealing his irritation, Michael had to admit that he was impressed.

Two world championship titles attested to Hakkinen's driving genius. He was one of those rare talents who always seemed to deliver ten-tenths while still leaving a small margin in reserve. He was also one of that elite handful who were prepared to go wheel-to-wheel with Michael Schumacher and sit it out with the German Ferrari ace and, had it not been for a crucial engine failure in the 2000 US GP, Mika might well have scored a hat trick of championships.

When Schumacher announced his retirement at the end of 2006 he freely admitted that 'some of his battles with Mika' were among his most pleasurable memories of his time in the F1 business. Compliments rarely come much bigger than that.

2005, 2006 Fernando Alonso (Esp)

b. 29.7.1981, Oviedo, Spain

87 Grands Prix, fifteen wins

Career span: 2001 (Minardi); 2003–06 (Renault)

It seems like only yesterday that he was the bubbly, fluffy young Spanish kid from Oviedo hanging around the Renault F1 team kitchens in 2002, helping the chef make pizzas on Friday afternoons. Then he was the team's test and reserve driver, twiddling his thumbs, frustrated at being on the sidelines.

Just a year had passed since he'd caught our attention in the Monaco media centre. An in-car cockpit shot of a Minardi popped up on the screen. The driver's hands were an unimaginable blur as he shaved the barriers with meticulous precision. Who the hell is this, we wondered? It was Fernando, his 20th birthday still two months away, laying down a marker for the future.

'For me, dealing with Fernando is like watching a movie for the second time', said Renault team boss Flavio Briatore, highlighting the similarity to his other protégé Michael Schumacher. 'No problem. Every time you see a movie you've seen before, you keep being reminded of little bits which caught your attention first time around.'

Pat Symonds, Renault's executive director of engineering, adds another perspective. 'The real similarity I see between the two is their self-belief', he said. 'Like Michael, Fernando has total conviction in his own abilities — he is able to see the target he has to reach, and to then go out and achieve it.

'It is almost as if these guys set a personal best every time they get in the car. I think it is characteristic of champions — and although I cannot prove it, I could almost guarantee that it would be the same in other sports — that ability to perform when it counts.' Small wonder that Alonso became the youngest F1 world champion of all time in 2005.

F1 Fathers and Sons

Gilles and Jacques Villeneuve

(Gilles: b. 18.1.1950; d. 8.5.82. 67 Grands Prix, six wins)

(Jacques: b. 9.4.71. 162 Grands Prix, eleven wins. World champion 1997)

This father-and-son combo made truly dynamic debuts on the F1 scene. Gilles drove a third McLaren entry in the 1977 British GP at Silverstone, immediately running with practised assurance in the top six until delayed by a faulty fuel pressure gauge. Amazingly, McLaren's not-so-shrewd management missed the opportunity to sign up the Canadian driver, with the result that he slipped through their fingers for 1978 and instead played out his entire F1 career with Ferrari.

Within the F1 community opinions always remained sharply divided as to Villeneuve senior's real status. Some judged him to be an instinctive driving genius, suffused with a quality seldom seen on the Grand Prix stage. Others regarded him as something of a hooligan who over-drove wildly in his efforts to force recalcitrant machinery to do his bidding. The truth may have been somewhere between those two extremes.

What all were agreed on, however, was that Gilles was very much his own man, an individualist in what — even by the late 1970s — had become a sea of conformity within the contemporary F1 community. His death was heroic. Stung by the treachery of his Ferrari team-mate Didier Pironi, who cheated him of victory against team orders in the '82 San Marino GP at Imola, Gilles was killed practising for the Belgian GP at Zolder a fortnight later. It was a mark of his status in his homeland that the Canadian government repatriated his body in a military jet.

At the time of his father's death, Jacques was eleven years old. He would grow into a resourceful and confident young man with a very independent streak. The younger Villeneuve has always marched very much to his own beat. In 1995 he won the Indianapolis 500 and was brought to Europe for an F1 test with the Williams team very much at the behest of Bernie Ecclestone. He proved impressively quick and, as team-mate to Damon Hill, started the first F1 race of his career from pole position. He came close to emulating the unique achievement of the late Giancarlo Baghetti, who won the 1961 French GP on his F1 debut, but eventually he had to give best to team-mate Damon Hill and settled for second.

Hill duly took the 1996 championship, but Villeneuve won it in '97 and then left Williams at the end of the following year to pursue the fortunes of British American Racing, a so-called 'dream team' which was built around him by his enterprising and resourceful manager Craig Pollock. The team would eventually be bought by Honda, and Jenson Button would eventually score their first race win in the 2006 Hungarian GP. Irony of ironies, this race also marked the apparent end of Jacques's F1 career as he was stood down from the BMW-Sauber squad after an accident in the previous Sunday's German race at Hockenheim. It was a poignant note indeed.

Mario and Michael Andretti

(Mario: b. 28.2.1940. 128 Grands Prix, twelve wins. World champion 1978)

(Michael: b. 5.10.62. Thirteen Grands Prix, no wins)

Mario Andretti will probably go down as the most versatile professional racing driver in the history of the sport. Not only was he an accomplished performer on the US oval circuits, both in Champcar and NASCAR machinery, but he was an accomplished long-distance sports car racer and FI ace of such capability that he won the 1978 world championship driving for the legendary Colin Chapman's Lotus squad.

Mario started his FI career from pole position in the Lotus 49B at the 1968 US GP at Watkins Glen, and fourteen years later would also be on pole for the Italian GP at Monza driving a Ferrari 126C2 turbo — where he posted the final finish of his FI career with a strong third place.

Michael was sixteen when his father won the world championship, and he would grow up into an energetic rival and sometime team-mate to his father on the US Champcar scene. In 1993 McLaren decided to take a gamble on recruiting Michael to succeed Gerhard Berger as Ayrton Senna's team-mate. On the face of it his credentials were impeccable.

Since his debut in Champcar racing in 1984, Michael had won 27 races and achieved an equal number of pole positions. In 1992 he had led the Indy 500 for 161 of its 200-lap distance before mechanical failure intervened.

Nevertheless, when McLaren boss Ron Dennis stood up at a media conference at the 1992 Italian GP, the overwhelming feeling was that the team principal was being unrealistically optimistic.

'I think he can win Grands Prix and become world champion', he predicted. 'It's not a question of which country you come from, it's how you demonstrate that desire to win. You've got to have that desire to win, and the aggression in traffic. There are probably less than five drivers who have that necessary aggression.' Even to those of us within the media pack who were willing those words to be true, Dennis seemed to be bordering on the reckless in his predictions.

Mario chipped in with additional, loyal parental support. 'I tell you, Michael in traffic is awesome', he said. 'He goes for gaps that I wouldn't even think about.' The problem, of course, was that Michael did not know the calibre of his opposition. Or their personal foibles.

The British driver Mark Blundell, then driving for the Ligier team, put Michael's dilemma into sharp perspective. 'In the British Grand Prix at Silverstone we were all racing for the first corner when I saw Michael pulling level with Jean Alesi's Ferrari. Now Jean wasn't a driver who was about to be intimidated by anybody, so he just braked even later. There was nowhere left for Michael to go except straight on into the gravel trap.'

Yet it was newly introduced restrictions on the number of laps which could be covered in GP qualifying and practice which really hurt Michael's efforts. Three races before the end of the season he was replaced by Mika Hakkinen, and that was the end of the sad experiment.

GRAHAM AND DAMON HILL

(Graham: b. 17.2.1929; d. 29.11.1975. 176 Grands Prix, fourteen wins. World champion, 1962, 1968)

(Damon: b. 17.9.1960. 115 Grands Prix, 22 wins. World champion 1996)

In their own separate ways they were self-made men. Graham was the self-taught mechanic who made good and scaled the peaks of the F1 big time while Damon, it could be said, created and crafted his own career out of the chaotic circumstances which followed in the wake of Graham's famous death in an aircrash one foggy night in November 1975.

While Gilles Villeneuve was killed when Jacques was a child and Mario Andretti had the satisfaction of watching Michael grow to adulthood, Damon lost his father at the difficult age of fifteen, an awkward adolescent turning point for many youngsters. Any opportunity for man-to-man bonding between the two was cruelly snatched away.

Damon was just two years old when his father won the 1962 world championship driving for BRM, less than six when Graham won the Indy 500 at his first attempt, and coming up to eight when he took his second title crown for Lotus in 1968. Graham was a complicated and proud individual who was branded as selfish and self-absorbed by his critics. Certainly the inner steel which helped Graham drag himself up by his bootstraps from his roots in suburban anonymity to achieve international fame and fortune had a less appealing spin-off in terms of a stormy side to his personality.

He could be crushingly and dismissively rude, even to those close to him. But his mask was never allowed to slip for his adoring public, for whom the suave image and saucy grin was all part of the projected persona of the archetypal sporting British gentleman sallying forth to take on the foreign marauding hordes. No question about it, Graham was quite a driver, even though the perception was of his being cast in something of a supporting role to the great Jim Clark, much as Damon would come to be regarded in relation to Michael Schumacher a generation later.

Yet much as we admire this father and son for their on-track motor racing exploits, their greatest contributions both came when they stepped up to the plate to stiffen the

Graham Hill

competitive resolve of two of the sport's greatest teams when they were beset by tragedy. In 1968 Graham helped Lotus pull itself together again after being rocked by the death of Jim Clark in a minor league F2 race at Hockenheim. Some 26 years later Damon would do the same to help Williams regroup in the aftermath of Ayrton Senna's death at Imola.

Arguably Damon's achievement was the greater of the two, even if he failed to emulate his father's '68 championship success. The key difference, of course, was that Clark's accident came at a time when death was very much taken in motor racing's stride. By the time Senna left us, that situation had dramatically and decisively changed.

McLaren-Mercedes MP4-21 Design Time Line

Stating the obvious it may be, but contemporary F1 cars are complex pieces of kit, and a bloke doesn't just sit down in front of his drawing board one afternoon saying: 'Right, I'm going to design next year's car in the next couple of hours.' Any such machine represents a snapshot of a particular team's accumulated technical knowledge as frozen at one particular moment in time. This time line on the development of the McLaren F1 challenger was prepared with the assistance of the team and published in *The Guardian* prior to the start of the 2006 world championship season.

First engine design meeting: .... August 2004

Engine specification first issue: .... October 2004

Layout work started on MP4-21: .... April 2005

First design meeting: .... April 2005

Gearbox simulation: .... mid-April 2005

Car specification first issue: .... May 2005

First scheming of gearbox: .... May 2005

First dyno test for V8 engine: .... June 2005

Wind tunnel work commences: .... early July 2005

First drawing for gearbox: .... July 2005

Datum sheet Issue, final dimensions: August 2005

First track test for V8 engine: .... September 2005

Gearbox production begun: ..... September 2005

Chassis manufacturing begun: ..... October 2005

Car mock-up ready:

    chassis .... November 2005

    initial engine .... November 2005

    final engine .... December 2005

Driver seat fittings:

    Pedro de la Rosa .... November 2005

    Juan Pablo Montoya .... November 2005

    Kimi Raikkonen .... December 2005

    Gary Paffett .... January 2006

First chassis ready for bonding: .. December 2005

FIA test on first chassis: .... December 2005

First car build started: .... December 2005

First full power gearbox dyno test: .. January 2006

First car build finished: .... January 2006

First track test of MP4-21: .... January 2006

Final shakedown before first race: .... March 2006

Cars depart McLaren Technology Centre for first race: .... Friday 3 March 2006

Jonathan Neale, Managing Director of McLaren Racing, explains how the new McLaren-Mercedes MP4-21 has gone from first concept to 2006 title challenger:

INTRODUCTION

When McLaren's engineers turn on their work stations every day, the first thing they see is a second-by-second countdown to the moment the four red lights go out to signal the start of the Bahrain Grand Prix. It is a stark reminder to us all of what we're in business to do — and the extreme deadlines we work to. If you worked in the road car industry you might see the results of your endeavours take several years to be translated into an end product. For the MP4-21 we're talking about six to nine months. So there's a hustle and pace about the factory which generates quite a buzz.

You might think the MP4-21 looks very similar to last year's car — apart, of course, from its striking new colour scheme — but in reality under the skin it is totally new. One single car contains an amazing 11,500 components, of which the carry-over from last year's car is typically less than 5 per cent. And that's not even including the engine — our colleagues at Mercedes-Benz are also dealing with 3,500 to 4,000 components within each individual engine. Combining all these into one quick car is a formidable challenge which started about eighteen months ago.

August 2004

Generally the Mercedes engine programme precedes McLaren's chassis development by about seven months, so the first engine design meetings for the 2006 car are held before the 2004 season is even nearly finished. Over the coming months Mercedes will work to give us the mass, centre of gravity, heat rejection and predicted power figures for the 2.4-litre V8. These allow us to start thinking how best to install the engine in the chassis and integrate it with the car's electronic and hydraulic systems which control everything from semi-automatic gearchanges to power steering to engine management.

April 2005

Our first design meeting for the MP4-21 chassis is held. The regulation change from a 3-litre V10 engine to a 2.4-litre V8 revving at around 19,500rpm creates a whole new packaging challenge; the different sized engine, of course, but also issues such as different sorts of vibration and the need to re-package the hydraulics and control systems. The discussions centre on what we've learned from the previous car, the MP4-20, and how best to incorporate those lessons in the context of the changed regulations — not just the engine but the multiple tyre changes and new qualifying system. We're determining what the wheelbase is going to be, establishing the airflow through the car to cool the engine. It's a time for optimising the design and making endless engineering trade-offs, such as chassis stiffness (a good thing) for extra weight (bad) and heat extraction for aerodynamic drag.

JUNE 2005

First dynamometer test for the new 2.4-litre engine, assessing its performance over lengthy periods on a static test rig.

JULY 2005 (first week)

Our first drawing of the new gearbox is completed. We'll make about twelve gearboxes over the course of the year. If you count all the nuts, bolts, washers, gear ratios (cogs), bearings and so on in a single gearbox, you're talking in terms of 1,500 components. That includes a choice of between 80 and 100 gear ratios. This extreme cutting-edge technology delivers us a gearchange time of a few tenths of a millisecond once the driver has pulled the paddle on the steering wheel — literally faster than the blink of an eye. The pressure in the design office is relentless. It's a race against time as we bring thousands of components together to build a new car in about 3.5 months, which after manufacture still only leaves us something like 30 full days of testing before the first Grand Prix.

JULY 2005 (second week)

Now the wind tunnel work starts in earnest. As a motor racing organisation we need to have a firm base knowledge of what makes a competitive car. Research and development is a seamless process and our wind tunnel, next door to the technical centre, is running 24 hours a day, every day of the week. We do a tremendous amount of simulation work, using computational fluid dynamics as well as all the air flow tests. By the end of July we're thinking in terms of harvesting all that base knowledge. At around the same time we also release what's called a 'wetted surface model' — the provisional outer shell of the car which is touched by the moving air — from the aerodynamic into the design department. At this point the chief designer has to catch the ball, because he's given what amounts to a slippery envelope into which he's got to shoehorn all the mechanical elements of the car. This includes the suspension, cooling systems, electronics, engine and more. By this stage there's a huge buzz in the technical centre developing around the new car, but we're releasing it into the design system just as the current racing season is approaching its climax in terms of pressure. It's a nerve-wracking time, to say the least! There's always a bit of creative tension between the aerodynamic and design departments, too, because there's pressure to finalise the shape of the gearbox's carbon fibre outer casing just as the design team are thinking how they'll integrate the rear suspension which attaches to the gearbox casing and so affects its shape.

September 2005 (first week)

First track test of the new Mercedes FO108S V8 engine takes place installed in an 'interim' (updated 2005) car.

September 2005 (second week)

Gearbox production begins.

October 2005 (first week)

Chassis manufacturing begins. Each one costs in the region of $250,000, excluding engine and gearbox.

November 2005

Juan Pablo Montoya and test driver Pedro de la Rosa attend our Woking factory for seat fittings. Having the driver fitting as comfortably as possible in the car is as crucial as tailoring the car's handling to their own personal preference. In that area, Kimi and Juan Pablo have such significantly different tastes. So the seats, pedals and headrests are all different. We also have all the necessary components — springs and anti-roll bars — to accommodate 50 different variations in car set-up, from very stiff to very soft.

December 2005 (first week)

Kimi Raikkonen visits the factory for his seat fitting.

DECEMBER 2005 (third week)

One of the MP4-21 chassis is tested to destruction as it undergoes the mandatory FIA impact tests. A huge sled with a lump of concrete on the end slams into the front, rear and side of the car. In road car terminology, it's a process of validation for the car type. It's a very stressful time because of the 'what if?' factor. What if you've miscalculated and the chassis implodes? You're back to square one but at a stage where you're well into building the second, third and fourth chassis ... Fortunately the impact tests all go OK — although as an engineer, watching the videos of this beautiful chassis on which we've expended so much effort being reduced to a cloud of powdered vapour still comes as a bit of a shock!

JANUARY 2006 (second week)

Our new British test driver Gary Paffett attends factory for his seat fitting. The first track test of the full MP4-21 package takes place at Barcelona with de la Rosa at the wheel. Even before the car's first run we have aerodynamic improvements and engine performance upgrades in the pipeline for the first Grand Prix in Bahrain.

28 February 2006

The car's final shakedown before first race is carried out.

3 March 2006

Three ready-to-run cars weighing 0.5 ton each – plus 33 tons of spares – depart from the McLaren Technology Centre for the opening round of the world championship in Bahrain.

Beyond the first race

The design department doesn't go on holiday once the cars are racing. During the Grand Prix season we'll be introducing technical changes every twenty minutes of each working week, with the aim of picking up about 2.5 seconds a lap from the first to last race, which is the sort of improvement you've got to aim for to be a serious championship contender. Put another way, to put two cars on the starting grid nineteen times a year we're making 6,000 new components every week.

THE FIVE ELEMENTS OF A QUICK CAR

There are five key elements to building and racing a successful Formula 1 car.

The chassis, in terms of its weight, stiffness and aerodynamic package, is a fundamental performance differentiator. The engine is the second key; you always want more power. The third is the tyres; you need to turn that power into grip.

Then there's the drivers. Physics will determine the performance envelope of the car, but the drivers determine what you get from it. So making a car which is very nervous, very peaky, isn't necessarily going to provide the fastest way round the circuit if the driver hasn't got the confidence to lean on it in fast corners.

Finally there is qualifying and race strategy, which is constantly changing and backed now by armies of maths graduates from the best universities in the country.

So when it comes to challenging for the world title we deal in a number of phases. But if the basic car concept is flawed, no matter what we do to compensate it will never be a winner.

MP4-21 IN NUMBERS

7 .... number of complete cars built during the season

12 .... gearboxes built over the year

20 .... number of minutes between each technical upgrade

11,500 .... number of components in each chassis, excluding the engine

4,000 ..... components in each Mercedes engine

MICYCLE THE BICYCLE

That was Mike Hailwood's nickname, bestowed on him by Jackie Stewart in the early 1970s. But to generations of reverential motorcycle enthusiasts he would simply be 'Mike the Bike'. Not only was he one of the greatest competitors ever to race on two wheels, but he was also one of nature's gentlemen, a guy with

no side who played down his celebrity status
with great charm and style.

Mike's switch to cars was never attended by
the sort of success he'd enjoyed on bikes. He
tried his hand in F1 with a private Lotus-BRM
run by the independent Parnell Racing team
during 1964, but it was a bit of a half-hearted
effort. Mike was reaching the zenith of his
career on two wheels and there was always the
feeling that he wasn't totally convinced about
car racing. Compared with the camaraderie
of the motorcycle world, he found F1 – when
he returned to it in the early 1970s – inhos-
pitable and unwelcoming.

'I've never seen so many miserable
bastards all earning £250,000 a year in one
place before', he once memorably observed.

Mike was a tough nut on the track, but
he was also a hero. In the 1973 South African
GP he leapt from his Surtees F1 car to help
rescue Clay Regazzoni from his blazing BRM;
a singular act of bravery for which he would
receive the George Medal. Later that year he
would be racked with guilt that he – and most
of his colleagues – failed to stop and offer
assistance to Roger Williamson, the young
British driver struggling to escape from his

upended, blazing March 731 in the Dutch GP.
Roger died in the inferno despite the brave
efforts of his rival David Purley.

Mike's F1 career ended after he crashed
his works McLaren M23 in the 1974 German
GP at Nürburgring, suffering badly broken
ankles. He seemed destined for a long and
happy retirement, but in 1981, on a trip to
buy a fish and chip supper for his family at
their home in Warwickshire, he was killed in
a banal road accident. His young daughter
Michelle died with him, but his son David
escaped unhurt. The rest of us were left
open-mouthed with disbelief. He was just
40 years old.

MEETING ENZO FERRARI

I was admitted but once to the presence of
the legendary Enzo Ferrari. A few days before
the 1986 Italian GP at Monza a small group
of us were invited to make a detour to his
Maranello lair, where we would be received by
the great man. Even the cynical downed tools
to be there.

Although he was then 88 years old and

entered the room assisted by his son Piero
Lardi, we were all struck by the aura of power
he radiated. Unquestionably, this man was
somebody. Yet his patrician image was an
illusion: he came from the humblest of
backgrounds. The force of his personality had
been moulded, developed and honed with the
passing of the years. His very existence, the
fact that he was a survivor from the pioneering
days of the sport, guaranteed that others
respected him as an icon. In so many ways he
seemed a prisoner of his own image.

In truth, Enzo Ferrari was a theatrical
gambler who played for high stakes, never
seriously believing he could come unstuck.
Having built up his Scuderia with the support
of Alfa Romeo during the 1930s, he had no
compunction about turning his back on the
Milan-based car maker after a dispute over the
management of the racing programme. He
walked out of the door in 1939.

Twelve years later Froilan Gonzalez would
win the British GP at Silverstone in a Ferrari
375, beating the Alfa Romeo 158s fair and
square in a straight fight. Immediately afterwards Ferrari sent the Alfa management an
emotional telegram, the contents of which
have passed into motor racing folklore. It

read: 'I still feel for our Alfa the adolescent tenderness of first love.'

To be frank, having met the man, that message sounded like over-hyped emotional claptrap. Old Man Ferrari struck me as one tough, unsentimental character to whom there was only winning. Hell, he admitted that one of his heroes was Margaret Thatcher.

Or was he, as with Alfa Romeo, just telling his audience what he thought they wanted to hear?

PRESSING COLIN CHAPMAN'S BUTTON

In many ways it was a decision which heralded the death knell of engineering initiative in the F1 business. When Colin Chapman, the dynamic Lotus boss, came up with the famous 'twin chassis' Lotus 88 it looked like the neatest of technical solutions.

The result of Chapman's deliberations was a novel design whereby the aerodynamic loads were absorbed by an 'outer chassis' linked to the bottom of the suspension uprights by a small coil spring/damper, while the driver remained housed in a central monocoque, the conventional rocker arm suspension of which absorbed the dynamic loadings produced by braking, cornering and acceleration.

This innovative concept offered considerable advantages. Firstly the aerodynamic performance of the car would be cleverly stabilised. Secondly, the driver no longer had to be battered about by the need to run ultra-stiff suspension, thereby minimising the fatigue aspect. The car was first tested in November 1980, equipped with sliding side skirts and built around an aluminium monocoque. This was designated the type 86, but was subsequently re-worked into the type 88 at the start of 1981 when the ban on sliding skirts was initiated. The new car was also built round an ultra-light, ultra-stiff carbon fibre/Kevlar monocoque.

Yet the FISA, then headed by the fiery Jean-Marie Balestre, was waiting to ambush Chapman's clever concept. Through the medium of one of its notorious 'rule clarifications', the governing body reminded participants that 'any specific part of the car influencing its aerodynamic performance must remain immobile in relation to the sprung part of the car'.

After a couple of false starts, the twin chassis Lotus was banned, but Chapman wasn't going down without firing a devastating broadside, not only at the governing body, but at the rival teams whom he believed had connived with the FISA to get his new concept banned for good.

'We have witnessed the changes which have taken place in Grand Prix racing', the Lotus boss stormed, 'and unfortunately seen what was fair competition between sportsmen degenerate into power struggles and political manoeuvrings between manipulators and money men attempting to take more out of the sport than they put into it …

'If one does not clean it up, F1 will end in a quagmire of plagiarism, chicanery and petty rule interpretation forced by lobbies manipulated by people for whom the word sport has no meaning.'

Balestre — who could never pass a microphone without bellowing into it — sprang from his cage in a right old lather, announcing that Chapman had discredited the world championship and Lotus would be fined $100,000 as a result.

The whole 'twin chassis' saga was a devastating disappointment for Chapman, but he had more worrying issues on his hands. Behind the scenes he had been conspiring to defraud the government over development monies charged for re-engineering the catastrophic De Lorean sports car. Only his sudden death in December 1982 came between Colin Chapman, total disgrace and a lengthy spell in prison.

FRANK WILLIAMS: THE LAST HERO

Back in the mid-1970s Frank Williams's cars were always scurfing along at the back of the grid. He proved remarkably adept at juggling his creditors, fending off the bailiffs and generally running the team on thin air. But he could never pull off the big sponsorship deal. And yet he must have tried harder than anybody else in the pit lane. Frank always radiated a single-minded confidence and determination which, one suspected, would one day reap its deserved reward.

As a young journalist I was slightly intimidated by Frank's confident assurance.

While attending the F2 race at Sweden's Mantorp Park circuit in 1971 I complied unwaveringly with his breezy suggestion that I got up early on race morning to give him a lift to the circuit. This was a rare privilege and I felt honoured, overwhelmed even. It never occurred to me that Frank hadn't two pennies to rub together and couldn't afford a hire car.

Unlike some subsequent F1 team principals, Frank Williams was never just along for the ride. He never operated in the comfort zone at any stage during his career. During the cash-strapped 1970s he was always battling against the tide and that zeal never deserted him a decade later when his cars were running at the head of the pack as a matter of course. He never backed off, never took things for granted.

On one occasion in 1975, I made some minor criticism of the Williams team's efforts in a report for the weekly newspaper *Motoring News*. Back came an extremely terse letter from Frank saying: 'I'm not in this business to ponce around in the pit lane wearing expensive pullovers.' I sent back a craven apology. Frank responded with a soothing missive. 'I really didn't mean to accuse you of not taking us seriously', he said. 'Please come to lunch sometime. My wife is a very good cook.'

I'm not sure I ever accepted Frank's invitation to go to his home, but me and my colleagues have delighted in his convivial company on many occasions since. Of course, the turning point for Frank Williams came in 1979 when his brilliant chief designer Patrick Head came up with the superb FW07 ground effect challenger.

That same year Frank decided to run a second car and recruited the popular former Ferrari driver Clay Regazzoni to drive it alongside team leader Alan Jones. Clay was hugely popular, almost 40 years old and still good enough to justify a place in the F1 business. He also went down in history as the man who posted the Williams team's maiden Grand Prix victory in the British GP at Silverstone.

Jones dominated the race from the start, but a cracked water pump casting caused his car's Cosworth V8 engine to expire in a cloud of smoke and steam. On the pit wall, Frank glanced fleetingly at the stricken machine as it rolled into the pit lane before switching his gaze back onto the track, where Regazzoni was now equally well in command. Jones was out, so Clay's survival was now the most important thing on his mind.

As Regazzoni's Williams FW07 clicked off those final miles to the chequered flag, a huge wave of patriotic fervour seemed to envelop the enthusiastic crowd. Perhaps for the first time, Frank would appreciate how much support and respect he had from the ordinary race fans who seemed genuinely delighted that this outsider who'd struggled against the odds for so many years had at last made the big time. It was as if Southend United had dragged themselves into the Premier League and were now poised to win the Cup Final.

Suddenly it was over. Clay roared through the long Woodcote right-hander to cross the finishing line and the Williams personnel chased down the pit lane towards the podium, literally whooping with delight. Frank walked a little way behind them, his face flickering with an almost self-conscious grin. His team had done it. What once had been perceived as a rag-bag of FI also-rans had now scaled a significant, unbelievable peak. It seemed as though Frank could hardly take it all in, as though he wanted to stand still and allow himself to be swept away in the vortex of this unbridled emotion which had erupted all around him.

The Next Alonso? Or the First Heikki?

You've got to hand it to Flavio Briatore. When he was boss of the Benetton team he could see there was quite a bit of potential in a young German kid called Michael Schumacher. A decade later a nineteen-year-old Spaniard caught his eye and he duly took him under his management umbrella. Fernando Alonso didn't turn out too badly either, barnstorming to the 2005 world championship as the youngest title-holder to elbow his way into the F1 record books.

So what next? On the face of it, the answer looks simple: an engaging 24-year-old Finn called Heikki Kovalainen. Runner-up behind F1 man-of-the-moment Nico Rosberg in the inaugural GP2 championship during 2005, the boy from Suomussalami — that's no joke, by the way — forged quite a reputation as Renault's officially nominated third driver in the 2006 world championship. Alonso or his team-mate Giancarlo Fisichella would only have to slip on their soap in the shower for Heikki to find himself propelled straight into the F1 front line.

For the moment, however, the newest blond Finn on the block is content with his lot. There are many in the F1 community who believe that Kovalainen may even have a slight edge on Rosberg in terms of sheer talent. So was it something of a let-down this year when he found his career path steering him towards the role of simply a test driver?

'In the middle of last year when my management first told me the plan was to have a year in this role I obviously found myself hoping that perhaps there might be the opportunity to race, because that's what I primarily wanted to do', said Heikki. 'But then when we thought about it a bit more, it wasn't really such a bad idea. So it wasn't a big disappointment at all, hopefully a great opportunity for me to get into a good car and race for the year after.'

In essence, he believes that testing in a top

car is probably doing more for his F1 prospects than racing down the field at the wheel of an also-ran. 'It's quite a tricky situation, of course', he said. 'It can work going into a small team from the start. Fernando made it work for him [at Minardi in 2001] but the problem is that the gap between those kind of outfits and the top teams are so great that it's probably better trying GP2, as I did, then going into a top team for testing.'

That said, Heikki admits that he was pretty disappointed not to beat Rosberg to the GP2 crown last year. 'It was very frustrating, because I obviously hoped to win it', he admitted. 'We started off quite strongly and were pretty consistent throughout the year, but the others got stronger at the end of the year and we couldn't beat them. But it's not something I worry about anymore.'

So how does Heikki rate Rosberg, the son of the 1982 world champion Keke, given that the two of them are likely to be pitched against each other in future seasons as a pair of the sport's most likely rising stars?

'Nico's OK, I reckon he's pretty good', said Kovalainen with a measured twinkle in his eye, balancing a portion of deserved praise with an understandable caution. 'Obviously he's doing pretty well, but as far as I'm concerned he's just another competitor. Nothing more than that ...'

Like Nico, Heikki's career began on karts at the age of nine. He did ten seasons karting before moving into the British Formula Renault series where he took fourth place in the championship. A move up into F3 followed for 2002 and he took third in the British championship with five wins, three pole positions and three fastest laps to cement his reputation as Rookie of the Year. He also demonstrated strong form on the international scene with second place at Macao and fourth in the Marlboro Masters event at Zandvoort.

It's clear that Heikki is now relishing the role of test driver and admits that the challenge of running flat-out on an empty circuit, without the racing stimulus of competing against other cars, can be quite taxing. 'It can sometimes be a little difficult pushing yourself really hard, but you really must do, you have to get through it', he said. 'This is the only opportunity I'm going to get to drive a really great F1 car and I try to drive every lap as though I was on a qualifying lap.

'To a large extent I'm measuring myself against myself, if you like, but it's obviously very stimulating on the occasions that I get the chance to test alongside my team-mates [Alonso and Fisichella]. Then I'll be pushing myself to match their performance. I've got to do that all the time if I'm going to be sure of getting a race drive in 2007.'

Despite all this, Kovalainen still thinks it's mildly amusing that most people remember him only for beating Michael Schumacher and WRC top dog Sebastien Loeb in the 2004 Race of Champions celebrity challenge in the Stade de France in Paris.

'It's certainly surprising, because it wasn't a serious event, really, just a fun weekend where some F1 drivers happened to be around', he grinned. 'But it still surprises me a little bit that it still attracts so much attention, even though it's almost two years ago now.

'On the plane going down to Imola for the San Marino GP, one guy came up to me and said, "hey, you're the guy who beat Michael in the Stade de France". But it's for my single-seater driving that I really want to be recognised.'

In due course, nobody doubts that he will. And we'll see just how good he is when he partners Giancarlo Fisichella in the Renault squad throughout 2007.

F1 Costs Through the Roof

F1 is painfully expensive. Slashing testing is one of the elements at the core of Max Mosley's cost reduction plans for 2008, and the urgency behind such limitations is thrown into stark relief when you consider that Toyota's four drivers – Ralf Schumacher, Jarno Trulli, Ricardo Zonta and Olivier Panis – between them covered over 8,500 laps in twenty test sessions at six European circuits, a total of 39,000 km, during 2005.

At $1,250 a lap in fuel, tyres, brake pads and other consumables, you're talking huge outlay before you've even paid for an engineer's air fare, let alone the cost of transporting the cars all over Europe. It really is a case of making a bonfire out of $100 bills.

Talking of high spenders, one of the least

charitable jokes which did the rounds of the F1 paddock during 2005 was that Toyota had made a mistake in thinking there was only one Schumacher in the business. Certainly Ralf's former manager Willi Weber demonstrated his negotiating wizardry to brilliant effect in securing his man a superb long-term deal with the Japanese car maker worth around $20m a year.

Just to make your eyes water, these are the figures I calculated for *F1 Racing* magazine for overall F1 expenditure in 2005. Makes you think, eh?

WIND TUNNEL COSTS $107,200,000

McLaren-Mercedes	$15.93m
Ferrari	$15.55m
BMW-Williams	$14.91m
Toyota	$13.14m
Sauber-Petronas	$11.71m
BAR-Honda	$11.62m
Renault	$9.06m
Red Bull-Cosworth	$6.78m
Jordan-Ford	$5.1m
Minardi-Cosworth	$3.4m

RESEARCH & DEVELOPMENT $250,810,000

Toyota	$63.4m

McLaren-Mercedes $45.66m
BAR-Honda $33.4m
Ferrari $26.6m
BMW-Williams $22.5m
Renault $18.09m
Sauber-Petronas $15.03m
Red Bull-Cosworth $13.48m
Jordan-Ford $12.2m
Minardi-Cosworth $450,000

Car Manufacturing Costs $16,080,000

Toyota $2.8m
McLaren-Mercedes $1.99m
Renault $1.92m
Ferrari $1.8m
Sauber-Petronas $1.75m
BMW-Williams $1.65m
BAR-Honda $1.37m
Red Bull-Cosworth $1.25m
Jordan-Ford $800,000
Minardi-Cosworth $750,000

Operating Cars at Tests $493,110,000

Toyota $77.5m
Ferrari $75.75m
BMW-Williams $74.5m
McLaren-Mercedes $65.86m
BAR-Honda $54m
Renault $44m

Red Bull-Cosworth $37.5m
Sauber-Petronas $27.5m
Jordan-Ford $26.5m
Minardi-Cosworth $10m

OPERATING CARS AT RACES $243,240,000

Ferrari $37.28m
Toyota $29.71m
BMW-Williams $27.46m
McLaren-Mercedes $25.33m
Renault $25.09m
Sauber-Petronas $24.03m
BAR-Honda $23.24m
Red Bull-Cosworth $19.51m
Jordan-Ford $21.34m
Minardi-Cosworth $10.25m

TEAM SALARIES $413,470,000

Toyota $68.53m
McLaren-Mercedes $62.23m
BMW-Williams $57.05m
Ferrari $51.04m
Renault $41.80m
BAR-Honda $40.70m
Sauber-Petronas $39.60m
Red Bull-Cosworth $23.78m
Jordan-Ford $16.5m
Minardi-Cosworth $12.24m

ENGINE BUDGETS $961,000,000

Toyota $180m
BAR-Honda $170m
Ferrari $150m
McLaren-Mercedes $140m
BMW-Williams $137m
Renault $115m
Red Bull-Cosworth $18m
Sauber-Petronas $26m
Jordan-Ford $15m
Minardi-Cosworth $10m

DRIVER SALARIES $161,100,000

Ferrari $45m
McLaren-Mercedes $40m
Toyota $35m
Renault $18m
BAR-Honda $10.25m
BMW-Williams $5m
Sauber-Petronas $4.5m
Red Bull-Cosworth $2.5m
Jordan-Ford $500,000
Minardi-Cosworth $350,000

TRAVEL AND ACCOMMODATION $93,910,000

Ferrari $19.46m
McLaren-Mercedes $14.05m
Toyota $12.97m

BMW-Williams $10.05m
BAR-Honda $8.53m
Renault $8.10m
Sauber-Petronas $7.7m
Red Bull-Cosworth $5.72m
Jordan-Ford $4.86m
Minardi-Cosworth $2.47m

Corporate Entertaining $68,550,000

Toyota $11.5m
Red Bull-Cosworth $10.7m
BMW-Williams $10.00m
Ferrari $9.0m
McLaren-Mercedes $8.5m
BAR-Honda $7.05m
Renault $6.5m
Sauber-Petronas $3.5m
Jordan-Ford $1.4m
Minardi-Cosworth $400,000

Grand Total 2005

Toyota $494.55m
Ferrari $431.49m
McLaren-Mercedes $419.55m
BAR-Honda $360.16m
BMW-Williams $360.12m
Renault $287.56m
Sauber-Petronas $161.32m

Red Bull-Cosworth $139.22m
Jordan-Ford $104.2m
Minardi-Cosworth $50.31m

TOTAL **$2,808,480,000**

WHEN THEY WORE ANOTHER'S HELMET

• David Coulthard in Michael Schumacher's at '96 Monaco: David was troubled with misting problems on his regular 'bone dome', so borrowed one of Michael's spares for the race.

• Rubens Barrichello in Tony Kanaan's at '06 Monaco: the two Brazilians swapped helmets for the Monaco GP and Indy 500 for sheer amusement. 'I've always wanted to try the Indy 500', quipped Rubens, 'but now at least I can say my helmet has done it.'

• Jochen Rindt in Piers Courage's, '69 France: Rindt found his full-face helmet made him feel nauseous on the undulating Clermont-Ferrand circuit and borrowed one of his

friend's open-faced helmets, which made him
feel very much better.

• Stefan Johansson wearing Nigel Mansell's,
Detroit '85: Johansson's regular helmet had
been temporarily misplaced, so Nigel stepped
forward with a spare to help. Three years later,
Mansell's helmet would be in a Ferrari cockpit
on a properly contracted basis!

• Ricardo Zunino wearing Niki Lauda's,
Montreal '79: mid-way through Friday free
practice at the Canadian GP, Lauda
announced to team boss Bernie Ecclestone
that he wanted to retire. Niki left the track
immediately and journeyman Ricardo Zunino
was drafted in to drive the car. But it was at
such short notice that he had to use all Niki's
discarded racing kit. Rivals wondered: 'Niki
seems a bit off-form and erratic today.'

THE BEST DRIVERS NEVER TO
WIN A WORLD CHAMPIONSHIP

Stirling Moss, Carlos Reutemann, Ronnie
Peterson, Gilles Villeneuve.

WHY THEY LEFT THEIR TEAMS

The relationship between F1 teams and their drivers has inevitably been prickly and unpredictable over the years. Michael Schumacher's eleven-year love affair with Ferrari was certainly the exception rather than the rule, both partners seemingly taking strength from each other to develop into what, for many years, seemed to be an unassailable partnership. Yet such alliances seldom enjoy tranquillity and harmony. Stress fractures, unrealistically high hopes which are not realised, and straightforward breakdowns in personal relationships have so often conspired to end many driver–team relationships. Here we take a look at some of the most memorable partings of the ways.

INNES IRELAND FROM LOTUS IN 1961

Colin Chapman ran and ruled the Lotus team from the outset with a rod of iron. What he said went. So when the charismatic Innes Ireland scored the works team's maiden victory in the '61 US GP at Watkins Glen, you might have been forgiven for thinking that Chapman might be at least slightly appreciative.

Don't you believe it. Judging that Jim Clark would be a better long-term bet than the fun-loving Ireland — and he was right — Chapman rewarded him by dropping him from the Team Lotus '62 line-up. Cruelly, Innes learned of his dismissal from a third party as the Lotus boss couldn't be bothered to tell him to his face. Tough, or what?

Graham Hill from BRM in 1966

Graham drove for Lotus for the first couple of seasons in his F1 career, then switched to BRM for the next seven years. During that time he helped keep the oh-so-British team in business by winning the '62 world championship, and also posted a hat-trick of Monaco GP victories between '63 and '65, the third admittedly made easier by the fact that his arch rival Jim Clark was away winning the Indy 500 for Lotus.

Finally, at the end of '66, Graham was signed to join Jimmy in the Lotus squad. It was the first commercially-driven 'super team' of the contemporary era, backed by Ford who were bankrolling the development of the new

Cosworth DFV, which would make its debut in the back of the new Lotus 49 in the '67 Dutch GP.

Hill put it rather more drily. 'If I'd stayed at BRM any longer, I was worried they'd spray me dark green and stand me in a corner of the race shop during the off-season', he quipped.

Emerson Fittipaldi from Lotus in 1973

Emerson decided that he would leave Lotus at the end of 1973 after a confusion over team orders in the 1973 Italian GP when his team-mate Ronnie Peterson took the chequered flag just ahead of him.

'Ronnie and I were expecting a sign to change positions with fifteen laps to go, which would have kept my chances open of retaining the world championship', he explained. 'So the signal didn't come and for the last ten laps we were both driving faster and faster, both right on the limit, but with Ronnie unable to get away and me unable to pass him. After the race I told Colin [Chapman] I was very disappointed, but he just said nothing to me. I think that's when I decided that I would go to McLaren.'

— Niki Lauda from Ferrari, 1977 —

After pulling out of the '76 Japanese GP at Fuji, Niki Lauda was very much a marked man at Ferrari. Some senior members of the Maranello squad believed he was a busted flush after surviving his fiery accident at Nürburgring the previous summer, and there was even a move to try to persuade him to take over the role of team manager.

Lauda wasn't having any of it. Angered that his new team-mate Carlos Reutemann was being openly touted as the number one, Niki strained every sinew to reverse the trend. He was successful in his quest, won the championship and then walked out of the team with two races to go after signing to join Bernie Ecclestone's Brabham team the following year. He was particularly infuriated that Ferrari fired his loyal mechanic Ermanno Cuoghi, cutting him loose in America with no money and only an air ticket home, simply because he'd decided to follow Niki to Brabham.

Nigel Mansell from Williams, 1992

Nigel dominated the '92 world championship but was horrified when Frank Williams not only asked him to take a pay cut for the following year but also announced that his personal nemesis Alain Prost would be joining the team in '93.

This was all too much for Mansell's dignity to deal with, so he flounced off to the USA where he impressed everybody by winning the CART championship at his first attempt driving a Newman Haas team Lola-Ford. Prost duly won his fourth world championship, only to be confronted by his own helping of the Mansell medicine when Frank announced he would be signing Ayrton Senna for 1994. So Alain decided to call it a day and retire.

DAMON HILL FROM WILLIAMS, 1996

Throughout the summer it was increasingly being speculated that Hill's demands for a pay rise to around $10m a year for 1997 had been dismissed by Williams. Yet Damon's lawyer and manager Michael Breen remained publicly confident that a deal could be reached with Frank, and he expressed doubt that the team had already done a deal with Heinz-Harald Frentzen.

'I think it is fanciful speculation', said Breen. 'Damon has won six races and is well on the way to the world championship. Damon has made it quite clear that he wants more money if he is world champion and Frank has indicated he is prepared to pay more. It is a question of establishing where the line is drawn.'

Yet the negotiations never got that far. A brief telephone call at 12.10 on Wednesday 28 August 1996 brought Damon Hill's career as a Williams F1 driver to an end. Frank politely told Michael Breen that he was withdrawing from the contractual negotiations which had been continuing for a couple of weeks. Apart from explaining that the decision had nothing to do with money, Williams offered no other explanation. He also made it clear that he would not be getting involved in a debate with the media over how — or indeed why — he had sacked the best British F1 driver since Nigel Mansell.

JACQUES VILLENEUVE FROM WILLIAMS, 1998

Villeneuve won the '97 world championship and stayed on with Williams until the end of 1998. With his baggy overalls, wire-framed spectacles, unlaced driving boots and the laid-back demeanour of a university backpacker, he brought a defiantly independent streak to the Williams squad. It was attractive, up to a point. Yet Frank and Patrick Head, the team's technical director, increasingly found that Villeneuve was too spoilt and wilful.

The issue for Jacques was settled after he asked Frank for a pay rise from $8m to $12m for 1999 if he was going to renew his contract. Williams, never one for paying more than he had to, reckoned that $6m was nearer Jacques' market value, so they went their separate ways. The Williams team would be winning again in F1 in due course. Villeneuve went to British American Racing where he became very rich, but never again scaled the peaks of F1 success he had enjoyed up to that point.

RUBENS BARRICHELLO FROM FERRARI, 2005

At the end of 2005 Rubens Barrichello was allowed to call time on his Ferrari contract with a year still to run, as he had become tired of continually having to defer to Michael Schumacher. He had won nine Grand Prix victories during his time with the famous Italian team, but believed that now was the time to make his own focused bid for the title crown. And that, he judged, meant moving to a new team, in this case Honda.

Barrichello believed that his experience of operating with a team of Ferrari's status and resource would ideally equip him to help develop the Honda team into a winning force. Unfortunately his first season in the new role saw him comprehensively eclipsed by team-mate Jenson Button. A relief for Jenson too, one would have thought.

JUAN PABLO MONTOYA FROM MCLAREN, 2006

Juan Pablo Montoya's white-knuckle ride with the McLaren-Mercedes F1 team finally hit the buffers after the 2006 US GP when the 30-year-old Colombian was fired from his drive with eight of the season's eighteen races still left to run.

'Juan Pablo is an exciting driver and immensely likeable character who will undoubtedly make a successful transition to the NASCAR scene', said Ron Dennis, the McLaren chief executive. 'We have agreed that with so many things happening in Juan Pablo's life right now, he should take some time out of the car and prepare professionally and personally for the future.'

A tongue-in-cheek translation of what

Dennis really meant was: 'Montoya never came to terms with the fact that he was being thrashed by his team-mate Kimi Raikkonen. And he kept on crashing our cars, so I'm quite relieved that he'll be crashing somebody else's in the future.'

RECALLING THE CHAMPIONSHIP CLINCHERS

SURTEES ON MEXICO '64

There were three drivers in contention for the world championship when we went to the final Grand Prix of 1964, in Mexico, and all were British: Graham Hill (39 points), myself (34 points) and Jimmy Clark (30).

It was a long flight down to Mexico City with a lot of intermediate stops, but of course the calendar had far fewer races in those days, unlike the current fortnightly schedule. The season finale took place three weeks after I'd finished second in my Ferrari behind Graham Hill's BRM in the US Grand Prix and seven weeks since I'd won at Monza, a success which really kick-started my championship chances.

Graham was obviously in the best position, but the situation was that Jimmy could win the title if he won the race, and I finished lower than second, with Graham lower than fourth. I could win it if I won the race — and also if I finished second, with Graham not in the first three. The points system was all very complicated ...

The whole complexion of the race was changed by an incident at half-distance, when my team-mate Lorenzo Bandini ran into the back of Hill's BRM at the hairpin. Lorenzo recovered quickly, and continued in second place, but Graham's exhaust pipes had been damaged, and he had to make a pit stop.

Towards the end Clark was still leading, with Gurney second, Bandini third, and me fourth. But in the late laps a trail of oil began to appear around the circuit, and we all began to take peculiar lines, trying to establish who it was who had the problem. No telemetry in those days!

It turned out to be Jimmy who had the problem, and going into the last lap he was crawling. Gurney swept by into the lead, and I passed Bandini for the second place I needed for the championship.

Over the line we all went, and it took some time for it to sink in that I'd won the world championship — my eighth altogether, and my first on four wheels after winning seven motorcycle crowns riding for MV Agusta.

After the race I remember shaking hands with Prince Philip, who had been in Mexico for the Olympic Games, and at the official prize-giving I was presented with a beautiful gold Longines watch by the President of Mexico. That was more than I actually got for winning the world championship!

PROST ON ADELAIDE '86

Through 1986 I was pretty competitive, but my McLaren-TAG had much less power than the Williams-Hondas, and at some circuits it was difficult to stay with Nigel Mansell and Nelson Piquet.

Obviously, Nigel was the strong favourite, but I knew I wasn't all alone against him. For one thing, my team-mate Keke Rosberg said he would race for me, and I knew he was a man of his word. And then there was Piquet himself — he and Mansell may have been in the same team, but they were at daggers drawn ...

As well as that, Nigel was going for his first title, and I knew what pressures there would be on him. Nelson and I had both won the championship before. So I wasn't without hope.

When the race started, Piquet led at first, but soon my friend Keke went past him, and pulled away. I was right in behind Piquet, who then spun, so now I was second behind Rosberg. Everything was looking good — until my right front tyre punctured, and I had to come into the pits.

To be honest, I almost changed my mind before the race — if the others weren't stopping for tyres maybe I should do the same. But I knew after practice that I was quite marginal on tyres — and my car was always easier on tyres than the Williams, so I stuck to my original plan. And although my chances didn't look good when I got the puncture, in fact it turned out to be a stroke of good fortune.

I now had some ground to make up, and I caught Mansell, who was running in the third position he needed to become world champion, whatever happened to Piquet and me. Twenty laps from the end I passed him — and as I did so, I noticed Rosberg, standing by his car at the trackside. Although I couldn't see it, his McLaren had a shredded tyre.

When I had stopped with my puncture,

the Goodyear people looked at the other tyres taken from my car, and concluded that Piquet and Mansell would be able to make the finish without a tyre change. They said that to the Williams people in the pits — but now, with Rosberg having a tyre failure, it was panic stations. Mansell was immediately called into the pits — but he never made it. A rear tyre blew on the main straight, and he had a big fight to bring the car to a stop in the run-off area.

Nigel was gone, but Piquet was still there. I pushed him, but he wouldn't budge, and I could hardly blame him for that! But he was still on his original tyres, and I felt sure he would have to stop. Finally, he did …

After I'd taken the flag, I knew my car didn't have enough fuel for a slowing-down lap, so I pulled up immediately, climbed out and simply jumped for joy. It wasn't my first world championship, nor my last, but it was the best day of my racing career.

LAUDA ON THE 1976 JAPANESE GP — *where he was pipped by a single point for the world championship by his close friend James Hunt.*

James was quite a guy. We were contemporaries as we fought to get our foot on the ladder in the early 1970s. Life was good then. James had a great zest about him and was always surrounded by a bevy of beautiful girls. I admired James for being a non-conformist. He got away with things that the rest of us didn't simply by having a lot of charisma. But he certainly was a formidable competitor.

It was quite a year for me. I'd won the first of my three world championships the previous year driving for Ferrari, but then I crashed and was badly burned in the German Grand Prix so I missed three races while totally focusing myself on the business of recovery. It was a pretty bad time for me, but I was lucky to have the right doctors at the right time and I was back on the starting grid for the Italian Grand Prix at Monza.

The Hesketh team, for which James had previously driven, closed its doors at the end of 1975 and for a few weeks it looked as though James might be out of a drive the following year. But he was too good for that to happen and, in the end, he picked up the plum McLaren number one seat after Emerson Fittipaldi made an unexpected switch to his family-owned Copersucar team.

Now he was in a McLaren, I knew James

was likely to be out to break my balls and, sure enough, he turned into my biggest opponent that year. But we still got on well and sometimes shared adjacent hotel rooms.

We went into the final race, the first Japanese Grand Prix at Mount Fuji, with me still ahead. I suppose on reflection I was feeling a bit tense after watching James eat into my points lead, a bit like I suspect Fernando Alonso is feeling at the hands of Michael Schumacher. I qualified third behind Mario Andretti's Lotus and James's McLaren, but then on race morning it started raining like you can't believe. We all stood around chatting amongst ourselves as the puddles built up all round the circuit and at one point it seemed as though the race might have to be cancelled.

Eventually, though, we started. I hit a puddle going into the first corner — got into a big slide — and suddenly thought 'I can't do this'. In my view conditions were just too dangerous. I pulled into the pits at the end of the opening lap where the Ferrari team wanted me to come up with some cock and bull story about suffering a problem with the car. I told them no, I was going to tell the truth. James finished third and won the championship, which was good for him.

DAMON HILL — *winner of the 1996 world championship at Suzuka*

Clearly Suzuka always has a special place in my memory, as not only was it the place where I clinched my world championship, but it was also the place where I set up my challenge for the title two years earlier when I was battling with Michael Schumacher and the Benetton team.

I always remember Suzuka as a very exacting circuit, although the paddock facilities were a little run-down even as recently as 1999 when I last raced there. And I understand that things are not much different today.

It is also a bit of a strange place in the sense that, because there isn't very much to do, the team personnel tend to gravitate to the paddock and hang around their offices perhaps more than they might at a European race. That makes the whole weekend more sociable and you tend to see more people around.

My first experience of Suzuka came with Williams in 1993. I was sitting in the pits waiting to go out when I was suddenly enveloped in a wave of jet lag which almost had me nodding off in the cockpit. I think I went straight out and crashed! Then in 1994 it was simply pouring with rain, a familiar theme in Japan, and I absolutely had to win the race and beat Michael if I was going to keep my championship hopes alive for the following weekend's Australian Grand Prix in Adelaide.

I just managed to keep Michael behind me all the way to the chequered flag, so that was a pretty satisfying day's work even though when it came to Adelaide there wasn't a happy ending due to my well documented brush with Michael.

Thankfully it wasn't raining at Suzuka in 1996 and the Williams FW18 I was driving was a really special car. I qualified second on the front row behind my team-mate Jacques Villeneuve, but I wasn't too worried as all I needed from this race to put the title beyond doubt was a single point, and I can recall sitting out on the starting grid feeling really content with myself and with what I'd achieved and thinking that, if it all went wrong at such a late stage in the year, then at least I was secure in the knowledge that I really couldn't have done more.

I felt really relaxed and serene, then took the lead at the start and won the race. It was a hugely exciting and brilliant note on which to sign off from my final year as a Williams driver.

BUTTON PROVED HIS
CRITICS WERE WRONG

By any standards, it was an amazing day. Jenson Button rounded off seven years' F1 endeavour and thwarted efforts in 112 world championship outings by breaking his run of disappointment to win the 2006 Hungarian GP, finally putting his name into the motor racing record book as one of the elite who have claimed their place on the upper step of the winners' rostrum.

He brought his Honda home 30.8 seconds ahead of Pedro de la Rosa's McLaren-Mercedes and the BMW-Sauber of Nick Heidfeld at the end of an afternoon which had been transformed into a wildly unpredictable lottery by heavy rain, which began falling just before the start of the 70-lap race.

The last eighteen laps were impossibly nerve-wracking for the 26-year-old in the mud-streaked Honda number 12. From the moment Fernando Alonso steered his Renault into the pit lane at the end of lap 51, this was a race which Jenson Button could only lose. Ahead of him was that narrow, twisting ribbon of tarmac which is the Hungaroring and just over thirteen seconds behind him the ominous scarlet nose-cone of Michael Schumacher's Ferrari.

On the pit wall the Honda crew monitored Button's progress. On the drying track surface Jenson's dry weather Michelin tyres were giving better and more consistent grip than Schumacher's Bridgestone rubber. As Jenson reeled off the laps, so Schumacher fell back into the clutches of Pedro de la Rosa's McLaren. Jenson just looked ahead, his senses razor sharp, adjusted to monitor every noise and vibration coming from his car.

By his own admission, Button didn't want it to end. But at the end of lap 70 it was over, and with the entire Honda pit crew lining the pit wall cheering, Button accelerated cleanly out of the final uphill 180-degree right hander and exploded out onto the straight to take the chequered flag.

From the touchlines Jenson combines a feisty outward demeanour with a well modu-lated inner confidence. He doesn't have that in-your-face confrontational competitiveness of a Nigel Mansell, yet he is perhaps less introspective than Damon Hill, let's say. What he does have now is sufficient experience to grasp the competitive nettle and play for high stakes.

Jenson Button's reputation in the F1 cockpit was riding high at the end of the 2004 world championship season. He'd finished third in the title points chase. Behind two Ferrari drivers. And he'd been on the podium on no fewer than ten occasions.

'I think Jenson did a fantastic job last year', said former Ferrari driver Eddie Irvine at the end of '04. 'He was really solid and never made any mistakes.'

But he added: 'Button's out-and-out pace we still have to ask about. If you look at his record against team-mates we know he's no Ayrton Senna. He's been beaten by every team-mate apart from Takuma Sato.'

That was biting stuff, but Irvine never pulls his punches. Yet his comments mirrored the widely-held view predominating the previous summer — that Button couldn't overtake. He nailed that lie in last year's German GP at Hockenheim, where he stormed from 13th on the grid to end up a splendid second. In 2005 Jenson clearly intended to leave the doubters in his dust in terms of raw speed as well.

Unfortunately it didn't work out like that.

The BAR-Honda squad got off to a slow start in the first few races of the year as they wrestled to get on top of the new 007's aerodynamics, and the first few races were a performance disaster. These were followed all too quickly by Jenson's disqualification from the San Marino GP and the team's suspension from Spain and Monaco after the FIA Court of Appeal following the controversy over the configuration of the car's fuel system.

Off track, Button's life was complicated by the need to unravel his 2006 contract with the Williams F1 team, a partnership he'd fought BAR to embrace only twelve months earlier but from which he now wanted to be liberated in the light of Williams' impending split from BMW. This turned into a protracted dispute, with Williams insisting that he required Jenson to abide by his contract for 2006, while the driver dug in his heels and made it very clear that he would consider sitting out that season on the sidelines unless he was released from his obligation.

This was hardly a state of affairs which could be expected to contribute positively to

Button's mental equilibrium, but if he allowed it to worry him at the races he concealed it well. Eventually a pragmatic solution was agreed, and Jenson bought himself out of the Williams commitment. But that eventual victory in Hungary made it all worthwhile for the likeable British driver.

HOW MANY RACES IT TOOK TO THEIR FIRST GRAND PRIX WIN

This one really makes you think. Giancarlo Baghetti won his first-ever GP for Ferrari at Reims in 1961 and, the best part of half a century later, that unique statistic remains just that. A unique statistic. OK, I hear you say, if that's the case why have you got Giuseppe Farina down as having won his first GP then? Well that's simple. Because the race concerned was the very first round of the official world championship back in 1950. Everybody and everything has to start somewhere, you understand. The bloke who came closest to emulating Baghetti's genuine achievement was Jacques Villeneuve, who started his maiden GP at Melbourne in 1996 from pole position, led for much of the race and then slid wide over a kerb — which damaged an oil pipe — and had to settle for second place. Not bad though, when, looking at this list, you realise just how long it took some of the greatest men in the sport's history finally to bag that elusive debut triumph.

So here we go with the list:

1st GP	Giancarlo Baghetti (1961 French GP, Reims, Ferrari 156)
	Giuseppe Farina (1950 British GP, Silverstone, Alfa Romeo 158; first-ever world championship GP)
2nd GP	Juan Manuel Fangio (1951 Monaco GP, Monte Carlo, Alfa Romeo 158)
4th GP	Tony Brooks (1957 British GP, Aintree, Vanwall; shared car with Stirling Moss)
	Emerson Fittipaldi (1970 US GP, Watkins Glen, Lotus 72)
	Lodovico Scarfiotti (1966 Italian GP, Monza, Ferrari 312)
	Jacques Villeneuve (1997 European GP, Nürburgring, Williams FW18)

5th GP   Froilan Gonzalez (1951 British GP,
Silverstone, Ferrari 375)

Clay Regazzoni (1970 Italian GP,
Monza, Ferrari 312B)

7th GP   Luigi Fagioli (1951 French GP, Reims,
Alfa Romeo 158; shared car with
Fangio)

Piero Taruffi (1952 Swiss GP,
Bremgarten, Ferrari 500)

8th GP   Jackie Stewart (1965 Italian GP,
Monza, BRM P261)

9th GP   Alberto Ascari (1951 German GP,
Nürburgring, Ferrari 375)

Mike Hawthorn (1953 French GP,
Reims, Ferrari 500)

Jacky Ickx (1968 French GP,
Rouen-les-Essarts, Ferrari 312)

Bruce McLaren (1959 US GP,
Sebring, Cooper T51)

10th GP   Luigi Musso (1956 Argentine GP,
Buenos Aires, Lancia-Ferrari D50;
Fangio took over car)

Mario Andretti (1971 South African GP, Kyalami, Ferrari 312B1)

Pedro Rodriguez (1967 South African GP, Kyalami, Cooper T81)

13th GP Damon Hill (1993 Hungarian GP, Hungaroring, Williams FW15C)

Jody Scheckter (1974 British GP, Brands Hatch, Tyrrell 007)

15th GP Jo Bonnier (1959 Dutch GP, Zandvoort, BRM P25)

Peter Collins (1958 Belgian GP, Spa-Francorchamps, Lancia-Ferrari D50)

Juan Pablo Montoya (2001 Italian GP, Monza, Williams FW23)

16th GP Peter Gethin (1971 Italian GP, Monza, BRM P160)

Ayrton Senna (1985 Portuguese GP, Estoril, Lotus 95T)

17th GP Jack Brabham (1959 Monaco GP, Monte Carlo, Cooper T51)

Jim Clark (1962 Belgian GP, Spa-Francorchamps, Lotus 24)

Denny Hulme (1967 Monaco GP,
Monte Carlo, Brabham BT20)

18th GP   Michael Schumacher (1992 Belgian
GP, Spa-Francorchamps, Benetton
B192)

19th GP   Phil Hill (1960 Italian GP, Monza,
Ferrari Dino 246)

Jochen Mass (1975 Spanish GP,
Barcelona, McLaren M23)

Alain Prost (1981 French GP,
Dijon-Prenois, Renault RE30)

Gilles Villeneuve (1978 Canadian GP,
Montreal, Ferrari 312T3)

20th GP   Innes Ireland (1961 US GP, Watkins
Glen, Lotus 21)

Gunnar Nilsson (1977 Belgian GP,
Zolder, Lotus 78)

21st GP   Lorenzo Bandini (1964 Austrian GP,
Zeltweg, Ferrari 156)

François Cevert (1971 US GP, Watkins
Glen, Tyrrell 002)

Stirling Moss (1955 British GP,
Aintree, Mercedes W196)

22nd GP René Arnoux (1980 Brazilian GP,
Interlagos, Renault RE210)

Dan Gurney (1962 French GP,
Rouen-les-Essarts, Porsche 804)

Peter Revson (1973 British GP,
Silverstone, McLaren M23)

Wolfgang von Trips (1961 Dutch GP,
Zandvoort, Ferrari 156)

23rd GP Vittorio Brambilla (1975 Austrian GP,
Osterreichring, March 751)

24th GP Nelson Piquet (1980 US GP West,
Long Beach, Brabham BT49)

26th GP Michele Alboreto (1982 Las Vegas GP,
Tyrrell 011)

Jean-Pierre Jabouille (1979 French
GP, Dijon-Prenois, Renault RS11)

27th GP John Surtees (1963 German GP,
Nürburgring, Ferrari 156)

28th GP   Carlos Reutemann (1974 South
African GP, Kyalami, Brabham BT44)

29th GP   Maurice Trintignant (1955 Monaco
GP, Monte Carlo, Ferrari 625)

30th GP   Fernando Alonso (2003 Hungarian
GP, Hungaroring, Renault R23)

James Hunt (1975 Dutch GP,
Zandvoort, Hesketh 308)

31st GP   Alan Jones (1977 Austrian GP,
Osterreichring, Shadow DN8)

Niki Lauda (1974 Spanish GP, Jarama,
Ferrari 312B3)

33rd GP   Graham Hill (1962 Dutch GP,
Zandvoort, BRM P57)

35th GP   Gerhard Berger (1986 Mexican GP,
Mexico City, Benetton B186)

36th GP   Didier Pironi (1980 Dutch GP,
Zolder, Ligier JS11/15)

Kimi Raikkonen (2003 Malaysian GP,
Sepang, McLaren MP4-17)

39th GP   Jacques Laffite (1977 Swedish GP, Anderstorp, Ligier JS7)

Olivier Panis (1996 Monaco GP, Monte Carlo, Ligier JS43)

40th GP   Ronnie Peterson (1973 French GP, Paul Ricard, Lotus 72)

41st GP   Carlos Pace (1975 Brazilian GP, Interlagos, Brabham BT44B)

John Watson (1976 Austrian GP, Osterreichring, Penske PC4)

47th GP   Richie Ginther (1965 Mexican GP, Mexico City, Honda RA272)

49th GP   Jean-Pierre Beltoise (1972 Monaco GP, Monte Carlo, BRM P160)

50th GP   Jochen Rindt (1969 US GP, Watkins Glen, Lotus 49C)

52nd GP   Heinz-Harald Frentzen (1997 San Marino GP, Imola, Williams FW19)

53rd GP   Patrick Tambay (1982 German GP, Hockenheim, Ferrari 126C2B)

54th GP   Elio de Angelis (1982 Austrian GP, Osterreichring, Lotus 91)

57th GP   Jo Siffert (1968 British GP, Brands Hatch, Lotus 49B)

62nd GP   Alessandro Nannini (1989 Japanese GP, Suzuka, Benetton B189)

67th GP   Felipe Massa (2006 Turkish GP, Istanbul Park, Ferrari 248)

69th GP   Patrick Depailler (1978 Monaco GP, Monte Carlo, Tyrrell 008)

           Riccardo Patrese (1980 Monaco GP, Monte Carlo, Brabham BT49D)

70th GP   Ralf Schumacher (2001 San Marino GP, Imola, Williams FW23)

71st GP   Johnny Herbert (1995 British GP, Silverstone, Benetton B195O)

72nd GP   Nigel Mansell (1985 European GP, Brands Hatch, Williams FW10B0)

81st GP   Eddie Irvine (1999 Australian GP, Melbourne, Ferrari F399)

91st GP   Jean Alesi (1995 Canadian GP, Montreal, Ferrari 412T2)

95th GP   Thierry Boutsen (1989 Canadian GP, Montreal, Williams FW12C)

96th GP   Mika Hakkinen (1997 European GP, Jerez, McLaren MP4-12)

110th GP   Giancarlo Fisichella (2003 Brazilian GP, Interlagos, Jordan-Ford)

113th GP   Jenson Button (2006 Hungarian GP, Hungaroring, Honda RA106)

117th GP   Jarno Trulli (2004 Monaco GP, Monte Carlo, Renault R24)

124th GP   Rubens Barrichello (2000 German GP, Hockenheim, Ferrari)

EVOLUTION OF THE F1
STEERING WHEEL

Time was when a steering wheel was just that: little more than a tiller with which to guide the car in a particular direction. Initially they were polished wood rims over light alloy frames, later evolving into leather-covered rims in the 1960s and 70s. But it was not until the evolution of semi-automatic gearchange mechanisms at the end of the 1980s — with fingertip-actuated paddle shift controls behind the steering wheel — that this essential component became effectively the control centre of the entire car's operation.

As you can see from the accompanying drawing of the steering wheel from the BMW-Sauber F1.06, almost every aspect and subtlety of the car's performance and behaviour is controlled by a switch or button which offers the driver instant actuation of every control dimension.

Back at the start of the 2006 F1 season, when Frank Williams was having a 'clear out' of what a used-car dealer might describe as 'stock surplus to requirements', he planned an auction and a lavish catalogue was duly prepared. A BMW-Williams steering wheel was temptingly estimated at 600 quid, so I devoted an *Autocar* column as to why all race fans should scrape together their surplus cash and bid for various items of FI memorabilia. Unfortunately the entire kit and caboodle was

I.	Pit Lane Speed Limiter	13.	Diagnostic
2.	Differential +	14.	Wing Angle Info Switch
3.	Engine Push	15.	Clutch
4.	Gear Upshift	16.	Differential Selective
5.	Traction Control +		Switch
6.	Engine Push Setting Switch	17.	Team Radio
7.	Clutch	18.	Traction Control -
8.	Traction Control	19.	Gear Downshift
9.	Team Info Inlap	20.	Engine Break
10.	Burn Out	21.	Differential -
11.	Multifunctional Switch	22.	Neutral
12.	Lambda	23.	Display Page Change

sold to a private buyer ahead of the sale, much to my disappointment.

Yet there was a nice surprise waiting. The next time I visited the Williams base, Frank most generously presented me with a steering wheel from Juan Pablo Montoya's Williams FW24. But as Patrick Head, ever the pragmatic engineer, shrewdly pointed out, the R&D costs of manufacturing such a component were probably around $10,000. But of course, without a car attached to the end of it, it was actually worth rather less ...

NUMBER OF WINNERS IN CONSTRUCTORS' WORLD CHAMPIONSHIP SINCE ITS INAUGURATION IN 1958

---

14 titles   FERRARI
1961, 1964, 1975, 1976, 1977, 1979, 1982, 1983, 1999–2004

9 titles   WILLIAMS
1980–81 (Cosworth engines), 1986–87 (Honda engines), 1992–94, 1996, 1997 (Renault engines)

8 titles MCLAREN
1974 (Cosworth engines),
1984–85 (TAG turbo engines),
1988–91 (Honda engines),
1998 (Mercedes engines)

7 titles LOTUS
1963, 1965 (Coventry Climax
engines) 1968, 1970, 1972, 1973,
1978 (Cosworth engines)

2 titles COOPER
1959, 1960 (Coventry Climax
engines)

BRABHAM
1966, 1967 (Repco engines)

RENAULT
2005, 2006

1 title VANWALL: 1958

BRM: 1962

MATRA: 1969 (Cosworth engines)

TYRRELL: 1971 (Cosworth engines)

BENETTON: 1995 (Renault engines)

Out to Lunch With a Star

François Cevert was a delightful, gregarious superstar with lashings of charm and charisma. Had he not been killed practising his Tyrrell for the 1973 US Grand Prix at Watkins Glen, he would have surely sustained the British team's competitive edge in the wake of Jackie Stewart's retirement from driving.

At the 1971 Easter Monday Formula 2 international meeting at Thruxton, I asked him tentatively whether I could interview him at some time for *Motoring News*. We were in the three-hour break between qualifying sessions, so when he said 'How about now?' I was more than a little taken aback.

'Fancy lunch?' he asked. Err, yes, I suppose so, I mumbled. So we climbed aboard his 6.3-litre Mercedes 300SEL, sped into Andover and enjoyed a convivial lunch in a local pub. Then François — still wearing his overalls — whisked us back to the circuit where he hopped into his Tecno F2 car and continued his business of the day. By 2006 the drivers would be so afraid of being mugged by gangs of freelance journalists they would never emerge from their motorhomes without an armed guard. Funny how times change!

Later in '71 I found myself in a Vienna *Bierkeller* with Cevert, Niki Lauda, Ronnie Peterson and my old friend Heinz Prueller, Austria's leading F1 journalist. Cevert brought the whole establishment to a halt by leaping onto one of the long polished wood tables and tap dancing the night away. Star quality? You've got it!

HIGH HOPES FOR HAMILTON

The arrival of Lewis Hamilton in the McLaren-Mercedes squad for 2007 as F1's first black driver has inevitably prompted huge interest and anticipation. When the official confirmation of his signing came through at the end of last year it was obvious food for one of my 'Racing Lines' columns in *Autocar* magazine.

In oh-so-many ways it will be the biggest ongoing story in British sport throughout 2007 as Lewis Hamilton makes history as the first black driver to arrive on the F1 starting grid. I just hope my friends at McLaren appreciate that their motorhome will be under media siege from the moment the personable 21-year-old resumes testing at Barcelona this week right through to next year's Brazilian GP at Interlagos on October 21.

The issue of ethnicity is obviously a fascinating element of Hamilton's emergence — and whether or not he can broaden the social appeal of F1 in the way that Tiger Woods has done for golf — but his recruitment to the ranks of the top-flight McLaren team is certainly no symbolic concession. Lewis has proved to be one of the most exciting talents to emerge in recent years and the almost paternal interest Ron Dennis has shown in his development reminds me strongly of the way he tutored Mika Hakkinen more than a decade ago.

Hamilton now stands on the verge of a bright new chapter in his career. But part of the McLaren education process will have drummed into him the obvious truth that F1 is different. It can grind down eager-eyed young talents and spit them out with a relentless lack of compassion if they don't match up. Squaring up to team-mate Fernando Alonso and going head-to-head with Kovalainen, Rosberg and Kubica, will simply serve to heap on the pressure.

Yet Hamilton's credentials are impeccable. In the junior formulae he did everything that was asked of him and more. It will be fascinating to see whether he can deliver in F1. And if McLaren can deliver the machinery for him to do so.

FAREWELL TO ONE
OF THE GREATEST

Michael Schumacher's retirement from the F1 business at the end of 2006.

We'd suspected it for months, but not until he'd won the 2006 Italian GP at Monza did we really believe the news. Michael Schumacher confessed that he would be retiring at the end of the year, during the course of a media conference in which he came closer to displaying his emotions in public than on any previous occasion in his career. It certainly struck something of a chord with me, as my 'Rumble Strip' column in the October 2006 issue of *F1 Racing* magazine may have conveyed:

> I've always been a bit of a sucker for romantic drama, so while many of my colleagues in the Monza media centre were looking aghast

as Michael Schumacher's voice faltered and he seemed to wipe away a tear, I was all set to start wailing with him. Why? I've really got no idea, to be truthful, but a good old dollop of pathos has always had me on the verge of blubbing like a baby ever since Rhett Butler told Scarlett O'Hara from the bottom of the staircase at Tara that he really couldn't give a damn.

Come to think of it, *Gone with the Wind* could really be a good title for Michael's autobiography should he ever choose to write one. But working out whether the rest of us could 'give a damn' whether or not he continued racing is a rather more difficult task. I wouldn't be impertinent enough to say that I ever considered myself as one of his closest friends, but on the occasions I interviewed him over the years he was unfailingly cordial, even though he knew well enough that I'd been a regular critic of his driving standards. Of course, such observations were water off a duck's back to this remarkable competitor driven by such compelling forces to be the best on each and every occasion he raced.

For all this, I felt privileged to be at Monza to hear the official announcement that one of the greatest drivers of all time had decided that it was time to park up and reach for his slippers. Yet the index by which Michael's status within our sport can best be judged is the reaction from the media in the wider world. For me, the news that Schumacher's retirement announcement took first billing in most German papers ahead of the Pope's visit to his Bavarian homeland really threw the whole thing into the sharpest perspective imaginable. This guy was clearly even more important *outside* FI than he was inside the business.

The sheer statistics of Schumacher's career fly in your face like a blizzard which threatens to overwhelm. Italy was his 90th win. He could quit with eight world championships to his credit. After Monza he had led an astonishing 23,667 racing kilometres in a career which had endured sixteen years thus far. His earnings over that time have been estimated at over 500m euros, a figured bettered only by Tiger Woods in the pantheon of international sporting stars.

Yet for me it is the small details which really stick in the mind about Michael. For almost 30 years now I have stayed in the blissful Hotel de la Ville in Monza, quite one of the very best locations on the FI championship trail. In recent times it has also become one of the Ferrari team's favourite haunts and to see Michael and Corinna tucked away on a table for two in the corner, untroubled by autograph hunters and totally absorbed in each other's company, has been both touching and reassuring in its sheer normality.

For all Michael's towering status as a sportsman, and his ruthless approach to his profession, he and his wife have always struck me as two people with their feet firmly on the ground, straightforward characters who have appreciated the trappings of wealth which have come their way and not obviously taking things for granted. After Monza, Corinna was quoted as saying about Michael's career: 'We had a lot of fun, they were great years for us. But now I just want him out safe.'

We should all be delighted for them both that Corinna Schumacher is on the verge of seeing her dream finally realised. They each deserve it beyond measure.

POSTSCRIPT: THAT MOST PAINFUL OF LESSONS

Don't get emotionally close to racing drivers. That piece of advice was offered to me by the late Denis Jenkinson, the famously controversial continental correspondent of *Motor Sport* during that magazine's heyday in the 1970s. The point was well made, but, of course, simplistic in the sense that you can't legislate for who you like and who you don't.

In the mid-1970s I was good friends with Tom Pryce, the young Welsh driver from Ruthin who won the 1975 Race of Champions at Brands Hatch in a Shadow DN5 and went on to put the same car on pole position for the British GP at Silverstone. Tom was a guy whose charisma was derived from a quiet and introspective personality which concealed considerable natural confidence and self-belief. His was a huge talent.

I spent a lot of off-track time with Tom and his young wife Nella and was very fond of them both. Then Tom was killed right in front of me in a horrifying and bizarre accident during the 1977 South African GP at Kyalami. Nella, suddenly a widow at the tender age of 22, faced flying back to London that same evening in an understandable state of shock. No counselling, no emotional assistance. Just a case of life is a bitch, so get used to it.

Eighteen months later, another friend,

Ronnie Peterson, was fatally injured in the Italian GP at Monza. That was it. I mentally closed my visitor's book, vowing I would never be touched by the death of a driver again. Silly really, but I was just 30 and had been to more funerals than my parents, who by then were in their early 70s. But, of course, I was kidding myself. When Gilles Villeneuve, Ricardo Paletti, Roland Ratzenberger and Ayrton Senna were killed, I found the tears again welling up in my eyes. Some I didn't know, some I didn't much like. But that, of course, was no reason not to be bitterly upset about their passing.

THOSE WE MOURN

The world was a much bigger, wilder place in 1968. On 7 April I was at Snetterton, reporting on a club meeting which *Autosport*'s then editor Simon Taylor had offered me five guineas to cover. Simon — who later went on to be Chairman of Haymarket Publishing — was thus single-handedly responsible for launching me on my ultimate career trajectory, an act of journalistic faith for which I shall be always hugely grateful. But that particular spring afternoon was preoccupied with events of more defining significance for the world of motorsport.

Jim Clark, the greatest driver of his generation, was killed that afternoon in a piffling little F2 race on the Hockenheim track near Heidelberg. And, I'm ashamed to say, my reaction was totally selfish and self-absorbed. Having written my report for *Autosport* and thrashed all the way down the A11 to London at the wheel of my mother's Morris Minor in order to deliver my copy, I then strayed down Fleet Street to where the early copies of the *Daily Telegraph* were being loaded up onto the delivery trucks.

I scrounged a discarded copy and read it by the light of a street lamp outside the *Telegraph* building. 'Jim Clark killed in Germany' read the headline. Oh no, I thought uncharitably. At last I manage to get involved in this business and now motor racing will be banned. That was the sheer scale — in my mind at least — of Jim Clark's passing.

Yet in the 1960s killing drivers was a routine facet of the sport. In consecutive months through the summer of '68, Mike

Spence was killed testing one of the Lotus turbine cars at Indianapolis, Lucien Bianchi died testing an Alfa Romeo sports car at Le Mans, and Italian hero Lodovico Scarfiotti was killed driving a Porsche in the Rossfeld hillclimb.

Happily that trend has changed very much for the better. The advent of carbon-fibre chassis construction, better safety barriers, and a more sophisticated — some would say enlightened — attitude towards circuit safety have ensured that most contemporary F1 drivers will be able to live on to a ripe old age.

Drivers Who Died as a Result of Accidents at F1 Grand Prix Race Meetings Since 1950

1954: Onofre Marimon (Arg) crashed his Maserati 250F practising for the German GP at Nürburgring.

1958: Luigi Musso (I) killed in his works Ferrari Dino 246 during the French GP at Reims.

1958: Peter Collins (GB) killed in his works Ferrari Dino 246 during the German GP at Nürburgring.

1958: Stuart Lewis-Evans (GB) died from burns sustained after he crashed his Vanwall in the Moroccan GP at Casablanca's Ain Diab circuit.

1960: Chris Bristow (GB) and Alan Stacey (GB) killed at the wheel of Cooper and Lotus respectively in the Belgian GP at Spa-Francorchamps.

1961: Wolfgang von Trips (D) and thirteen spectators killed at Monza when he crashed his Ferrari 156 on the second lap of the Italian GP.

1964: Carel de Beaufort (NL) died from injuries sustained when he crashed his 4-cylinder Porsche at the Bergwerk corner on the Nürburgring while practising for the German GP.

1966: John Taylor (GB) succumbed to burns after crashing his Brabham during the German GP at Nürburgring.

1967: Lorenzo Bandini (I) fatally burned after his Ferrari 312 crashed during the closing stages of the Monaco GP.

1968: Jo Schlesser (F) killed when his Honda RA302 crashed and burned in the French GP at Rouen-les-Essarts.

1969: Gerhard Mitter (D) killed after crashing at Flugplatz on the Nürburgring while practising his BMW 269 for the F2 section of the German GP.

1970: Piers Courage (GB) killed when his Frank Williams-entered de Tomaso 505 crashed and burned during the Dutch GP at Zandvoort.

1970: Jochen Rindt (Au) killed when his Lotus 72 crashed under-braking for Monza's Parabolica corner during practice for the Italian GP.

1973: Roger Williamson (GB) died after his March 731G crashed and caught fire during the Dutch GP at Zandvoort.

1973: FRANÇOIS CEVERT (F) killed after crashing his Tyrrell-Ford 006 during qualifying for the United States GP at Watkins Glen.

1974: HELMUTH KOINIGG (Au) killed when his Surtees-Ford crashed during the United States GP at Watkins Glen.

1975: MARK DONOHUE (USA) died from head injuries sustained when he crashed his Penske team March 761 in the race morning warm-up prior to the Austrian GP at the Osterreichring.

1977: TOM PRYCE (GB) killed after his Shadow-Ford DN8 collided with a marshal crossing the circuit during the South African GP at Kyalami.

1978: RONNIE PETERSON (Swe) died from injuries sustained when his Lotus 78 crashed at the start of the Italian GP at Monza.

1982: GILLES VILLENEUVE (Can) fatally injured practising his Ferrari 126C2 for the Belgian GP at Zolder.

1982: Ricardo Paletti (I) fatally injured after his Osella-Ford was involved in a start-line collision during the Canadian GP at Montreal.

1994: Roland Ratzenberger (Au) killed when his Simtek-Ford crashed during qualifying for the San Marino GP at Imola.

1994: Ayrton Senna (Br) fatally injured when his Williams-Renault FW14 crashed while leading the San Marino GP at Imola.

INDEX